Daily Beside The Still Waters

DEVOTIONS FROM PSALMS

Dr. Mike Smith

Franklin Publishing
PRINCETON, TEXAS

Copyright © 2020 by Mike Smith.

All rights reserved. No part of this publication may be reproduced, distributed or transmitted in any form or by any means, including photocopying, recording, or other electronic or mechanical methods, without the prior written permission of the publisher, except in the case of brief quotations embodied in critical reviews and certain other noncommercial uses permitted by copyright law. For permission requests, write to the publisher, addressed "Attention: Permissions Coordinator," at the address below.

Kelly Carr / Franklin Publishing
1215 Juniper
Princeton, Texas 75407

www.FranklinPublishing.org

Ordering Information:

Quantity sales. Special discounts are available on quantity purchases by corporations, associations, and others. For details, contact the "Special Sales Department" at the address above.

Except where otherwise indicated, all Scripture quotations are taken from the New King James Version®. Copyright © 1982 by Thomas Nelson. Used by permission. All rights reserved.

Daily Beside The Still Waters: Devotions From Psalms / Mike Smith. —1st ed.

ISBN-13: 978-1-7320028-8-3
ISBN-10: 1-7320028-8-6

Contents

Introduction to Psalms 9
Psalms Reading Plan 11
The 5 W's of Psalms 13
Day 1 19
Day 2 22
Day 3 25
Day 4 28
Day 5 31
Day 6 34
Day 7 37
Day 8 41
Day 9 44
Day 10 48
Day 11 51
Day 12 55
Day 13 58
Day 14 62
Day 15 66
Day 16 70
Day 17 74

Day 18	78
Day 19	82
Day 20	86
Day 21	90
Day 22	94
Day 23	97
Day 24	101
Day 25	105
Day 26	109
Day 27	113
Day 28	117
Day 29	120
Day 30	124
Day 31	128
Bibliography	133
About the Author	137

Dedication

L.C. Smith and Doris Ann Davis Smith were my parents. My mother died near midnight on July 30, 2017. Within 36 hours of her death, my dad died on August 1, 2017. From the time they met in rural Clarke County, Mississippi in 1949, they did everything together. My dad was a 19-year old logger with one log truck and a saw. My mother was a 16-year old, full of energy. Their place of courtship was in the log truck. They married on July 7, 1949. During the early years of their marriage, they moved at least once a month. My dad would log during the week, and my mother would cook meals for the hired hands. In between meal preparation, she would find another house. On Saturdays, they loaded the log truck and moved on to the next location. Both had a desire to better themselves.

In 1950, I was born, and we all headed to Oregon. Oregon was famous for its big trees, so my Dad thought he would make more money as a logger there. On our way to Oregon, we stopped in Houston, Texas, to visit Uncle Bob, who had moved to the big city earlier. In Houston, my dad saw his first oil well-pumping unit and was hooked. We never made it to Oregon.

Dad worked his way up from an oilfield "worm" to owning his own company. Cardinal Well Service was one of the largest independent one-owner well service companies in Texas. At one time, they had over two hundred rigs, trucks, and other vehicles for which the company purchased license plates.

My mother was full of laughter and enjoyed a variety of careers throughout her life. She became a licensed beautician and operated a beauty shop; she opened an antique gift shop; she designed and manufactured "Big Boy" children's clothes, and she worked in the Cardinal Well Service office. Most of her time, however, was spent playing bridge, hosting tea parties, shopping, decorating the church for special occasions, and having fun with friends.

My parents worked hard. God blessed them, and they were able to see the world and do whatever they wanted, but the last five years of their lives were difficult to see as their bodies and minds became more and more feeble. So, their dying within thirty-six hours of one another was a blessing. Earlier in their lives, they had both confessed Jesus as their Lord and Savior. They were devoted to each other, so this book of devotions is dedicated to them.

*"This is the day the LORD has made;
We will rejoice and be glad in it."*

—PSALM 118:24

Introduction to Psalms

Early in my Christian walk, someone challenged me to read the Wisdom Literature of the Bible. I was instructed to read five psalms and the one chapter of Proverbs for the corresponding day of the month.

This book is a devotional book to encourage you to read the psalms. Psalms are packed with praise, prayers, prophecies, and the pain and problems that we all experience in life.

This introduction will provide a brief background to Psalms. It will answer the 5 W's of Psalms – who, what, when, where and why. I will provide you with a reading chart to assist as you read.

Each day the format will be:

LISTEN TO GOD

Start reading the psalm that corresponds with that day of the month. Also, ready every 30th psalm. For example. On June 1, read Psalms 1, 31, 61, 91, and 121. Unless otherwise noted, all scripture references will be from the King James Version (KJV) Public Domain.

LEARN OF GOD

Record any thoughts you learn. This is not to be a detailed expression. Look for one word or thought that God impressed upon you as you read the psalms. Meditate on this throughout the day.

LEAN ON GOD

Remember to pray. Write out your prayer or spend time in prayer.

LAUGH WITH GOD

Read and share. I believe God has a sense of humor. It is healthy to laugh each day, even in the midst of pain. These jokes I label as "Lee Jokes." They are jokes from my friend, Lee Welch. I met Lee in 1978. Over the years, we have pastored together in the same association of churches, and at one time, he pastored the church where my family and I were members. We have traveled numerous times together to mission trips, conventions, and conferences. Laughter helps life go better, and Lee could always make me laugh. Yes, many of the "Lee Jokes" are corny, but they bring laughter, and we need to laugh.

Psalms Reading Plan

DAY	PSALMS				
1	1	31	61	91	121
2	2	32	62	92	122
3	3	33	63	93	123
4	4	34	64	94	124
5	5	35	65	95	125
6	6	36	66	96	126
7	7	37	67	97	127
8	8	38	68	98	128
9	9	39	69	99	129
10	10	40	70	100	130
11	11	41	71	101	131
12	12	42	72	102	132
13	13	43	73	103	133
14	14	44	74	104	134
15	15	45	75	105	135
16	16	46	76	106	136
17	17	47	77	107	137
18	18	48	78	108	138
19	19	49	79	109	139
20	20	50	80	110	140
21	21	51	81	111	141
22	22	52	82	112	142
23	23	53	83	113	143
24	24	54	84	114	144
25	25	55	85	115	145
26	26	56	86	116	146
27	27	57	87	117	147
28	28	58	88	118	148
29	29	59	89	119	149
30	30	60	90	120	150
31	31	119			

Dr. Mike Smith

The 5 W's of Psalms

WHO?

There are at least eight authors of the psalms. We know seven of them.
1. David – 3, 4, 5, 6, 7, 8, 9, 11, 12, 13, 14, 15, 16, 17, 18, 19, 20, 21, 22, 23, 24, 25, 26, 27, 28, 29, 30, 31, 32, 34, 35, 36, 37, 38, 39, 40, 41, 51, 52, 53, 54, 55, 56, 57, 58, 59, 60, 61, 62, 63, 64, 65, 66, 67, 68, 69, 70, 86, 101, 108, 109, 110, 122, 124, 131, 133, 138, 139, 140, 141, 142, 143, 144, 145. Acts 4:25 ascribes Psalm 2 to David. I believe David wrote 33, 17, 103, 104, and 132.
2. Asaph – 50, 73, 74, 75, 76, 77, 78, 70, 80, 81, 82, 83.
3. Sons of Korah – 42, 45, 46, 47, 48, 49, 84, 85, 87.
4. Solomon – 72, 127. I believe 128 belongs to Solomon.
5. Herman the Ezrahite – 88.
6. Ethan – 89.
7. Moses – 90
8. Unknown – 1, 66, 67, 87, 90, 91, 92, 93, 94, 95, 96, 97, 98, 99, 100, 105, 106, 107, 108, 109,

110, 111, 112, 113, 114, 115, 116, 117, 118, 119, 120, 121, 123, 125, 126, 129, 134, 135, 136, 137, 146, 147, 148, 149, 150.

9. Some of the suggested authors of these are:

   a. 77 – Habakkuk
   b. 90 – Moses, David, Hezekiah, Nathan the Seer, or Isaiah[1]
   c. 102 – Hezekiah, Daniel
   d. 106 – Daniel
   e. 119 – David, Hezekiah, Jeremiah, Ezra, Nehemiah, Malachi, Daniel
   f. 121 – Hezekiah
   g. 123 – Hezekiah
   h. 129 – Hezekiah
   i. 130 – Hezekiah
   j. 146 and 147 – Haggai, Zechariah

Ezra likely compiled all the psalms.

WHAT?

The Hebrew title for Psalms was *sepher Tehelim*, which means a book of praises or hymns. The word "psalms" is from Greek *psalmoi or psallein*, which means to play on a stringed instrument. In general, Psalms is a song book, poetic in form. It belongs to the 5 books of Wisdom, or poetic literature. Psalms is a book of Wisdom.

TYPES OF PSALMS

1. Lament: Songs of Sorrow

3, 4, 5, 6, 7, 8, 9, 10, 12, 38, 44, 60 74, 79 80, 83, 85,
89, 90, 94, 123, 126, 129, 13, 14, 17, 22, 25, 26, 27,
28, 31, 32, 36, 38, 39, 40, 41, 42, 43, 51, 52, 53, 54,
55, 56, 57, 59, 61, 64, 70, 71, 77, 86, 89, 102, 120,
130, 139, 140, 141, 142

2. Imprecatory: Songs to Invoke God's Wrath

   35 69, 83, 88, 109, 137, 140

3. Thanksgiving: Songs to Give Thanks

   65, 67, 75, 17, 124, 136, 18, 21, 30, 32, 34, 40, 66, 20,
   92, 108, 116, 118, 138, 8, 105, 106, 135, 136, 11, 16,
   23, 27, 62, 63, 91, 121, 125, 135

4. Praise: Songs to Sing

   8, 19, 33, 66, 67, 95, 100, 103, 104, 111, 113,114, 117,
   145, 146, 147, 148, 149, 150, 50, 78, 81, 89, 132, 46,
   48, 76, 84, 87, 122, 15, 24, 68, 82, 95, 115, 134, 1, 36,
   37, 49, 73, 112, 127, 128, 119

5. Royal: Songs to the King/Messianic/Prophetic

   2, 18, 20, 21, 29, 45, 47, 72, 93, 95, 96, 97, 98 99, 101,
   110, 144

English poetry relies on rhyme and meter to communicate the message. Old Testament poetry does not rely on rhyme, and scholars argue if the psalms have a meter or not. The two characteristics of Hebrew poetry are terseness and parallelism.

Terseness is expressing a complex thought in a few words. Example: "The Lord is my shepherd" (Psalms 23:1). The lord is my shepherd is a simple scene of a shepherd leading his sheep. Yet, when you think of Jesus as our shepherd, the picture is more complex. This is terseness.

Parallelism is when the second line of a verse repeats or advances the thought of the first line. There are different kinds of parallelism. Examples:
- Similar Parallelism: Psalm 139:1, "You have searched me, Lord, and you know me." The second line intensifies the first line.
- Contrasting Parallelism: Psalm 20:7, "Some trust in chariots and some trust in horses, but we trust in the name of the Lord our God."

WHEN?

The timeframe covers the entire Old Testament. It is likely that Ezra compiled the Psalms around 400 B.C.

WHERE?

Like the timeframe, the Psalms were written in the Wilderness of Sinai and in the King's Palace of Jerusalem.

WHY?

Every type of problem known to man is covered in Psalms. They provide conviction and comfort. They offer up praise and prophecy. Basically, Psalms was written as a songbook. Praises and laments are to be sung for comfort and cheer. The first five books of the Old Testament are also known as the law or books of Moses. Each of the Psalms corresponds to one of these books.

Psalms is divided into five sections or books, as follows:
- Book 1 – Psalms 1-41 – God's Sovereignty – Genesis
- Book 2 – Psalms 42-72 – God's Salvation – Exodus

- Book 3 – Psalms 73-89 – God's Sanctuary – Leviticus

- Book 4 – Psalms 90-106 – God's Sufficiency – Numbers

- Book 5 – Psalms 107-150 – God's Sermons – Deuteronomy 5

Psalms also reveal the life of Christ.

Psalms	New Testament	Application
2:1-2, 7	Acts 4:25-26; 13:33	Jesus is the Messiah
16:1-11	Acts 2:25	Jesus will rise from the dead
22:1-31	Matthew 27:35,46, John 19:24, Hebrews 2:12	Jesus will be forsaken
41:9	John 13:18	Jesus will be betrayed
110:1-8	Matthew 22:24, Mark 12:20, Luke 10:27, Hebrews 5:6	Jesus will rule as Lord and High Priest
118:1-29	Matthew 21:42, Hebrews 13:6	Jesus will gain victory over his enemies and over death

The writers of Psalms anticipated the life of Jesus, the anointed one, who would come later. This is especially seen in the Gospels.

Psalms	Jesus	Gospel
2, 24, 18, 47, 20, 110, 21, 132	The King	Matthew
17, 41, 22, 69, 23, 109, 40	The Servant	Mark
8, 40, 16	The Son of Man	Luke
19, 118, 102, 7	The Son of God	John

The key word in Psalms is worship. The word "worship" occurs fifteen times in the King James Version of Psalms.

Let reading the Psalms be a time of devotion and quiet communication between you and God. The words of God shape us. See, for instance Romans 12:2.

Notes

Day 1

LISTEN TO GOD

Read Psalms 1, 31, 61, 91, and 121.

WORD

Notice a common thread in these five psalms. We will not see this every day, but the connection is clear today.

Psalm 1:1-2, "Blessed is the man that walketh not in the counsel of the ungodly, nor standeth in the way of sinners, nor sitteth in the seat of the scornful. But his delight is in the law of the Lord; and in his law doth he meditate day and night."

Psalm 31:1, 3, "In thee, O Lord, do I put my trust; let me never be ashamed: deliver me in thy righteousness. For thou art my rock and my fortress; therefore for thy name's sake lead me, and guide me."

Psalm 61:1, "Hear my cry, O God; attend unto my prayer."

Psalm 91:1, "He that dwelleth in the secret place of the most High shall abide under the shadow of the Almighty."

Psalm 121:1-2, "I will lift up mine eyes unto the hills, from whence cometh my help. My help cometh from the Lord, which made heaven and earth."

The theme that leaps out in every one of these five psalms is the Word of God. This world will try to tear you down and destroy you. The Word of God will equip you to stand against the world. This is one reason why it is essential to start the day in His Word.

I have not always been consistent. I've started various devotional times and methods only to abandon them. But I am thankful that God always draws me back to a time in His Word. The Word refreshes me, renews me, and provides me with resources that I need to face the day. I challenge you to set aside a place and a time of fifteen minutes to read the Word of God and pray.

Christmas 2017 will always be a special memory for me. My daughter, Martha Elaine Smith-Gardner, gave me the Spurgeon Study Bible. Charles Hadden Spurgeon was one of my heroes. However, it is what Martha Elaine wrote on the inside cover that means so much to me. "Daddy, thank you for giving me a love for God's Word and teaching it to others. It is a gift I hope to pass on to my children. In every house we have lived in, I have a vivid memory of where you sat and read your Bible. I love you, Martha Elaine." I could leave my children a house, some land, or a certificate of deposit; but nothing would help them more than the discipline of reading ...

GOD'S WORD

LEARN FROM GOD:

Record one thing that you learned.

LEAN ON GOD:

Remember to pray that God will open your eyes of understanding as you read His Word.

LAUGH WITH GOD:

Read the following joke and share it with others.

Every morning, an elderly woman would step out on her porch, raise her arms to heaven, and shout, "Praise God!" An atheist happened to buy the house next door to her, and over the months he became very irritated with the spiritual woman. After six months of hearing her shout "Praise God" each morning, he went outside on his porch and yelled, "There is no god!" The godly woman wasn't put off in the least. She continued to praise God every day. One cold winter morning, the atheist heard the woman shout a different message. "Help me, Lord," the woman prayed. "It's very cold and I am out of food and money." When the woman went outside the next morning there was enough food on the porch to last her a month. "Praise God!" she shouted. The atheist stepped out from the bushes and said, "There is no god! I bought all those groceries!" The woman raised her arms to heaven and said, "Praise God! You sent me groceries and made the devil pay for them!

Day 2

LISTEN TO GOD

Read Psalms 2, 32, 62, 92, and 122.

FORGIVEN

"Blessed is he whose transgression is forgiven, whose sin is covered. Blessed is the man unto whom the LORD imputeth not iniquity, and in whose spirit there is no guile." Psalm 32:1-2

Indeed, it is a blessing to know my sins are forgiven. To live with guilt and shame is depressing. Because many live in a prison of guilt, they never experience true happiness. They carry memories or multitudes of words and deeds of which they are ashamed. *Imputeth* is a legal term. To impute guilt to someone is to assign guilt to that person's account. The guilt of sinners was imputed to Christ. Sin was imputed, not imparted. His character would not let Him be sin, but in the count of Heaven, He was imputed with our sin.

2 Corinthians 5:21 says, "For he hath made him to be sin for us, who knew no sin; that we might be made the righteousness of God in him."

Leviticus 16 describes the events of the Day of Atonement. On this day, the High Priest first took the blood of bulls, entered the Holy of Holies, and sprinkled the blood on the mercy seat sever times. This covered his sins. Next, he took the blood of bulls and sprinkled it on the mercy seat seven more times, and then he sprinkled blood on the golden altar and the horns of the altar. This covered the sins of the people. This was a picture of Christ who was to come. Hebrews 9:11-14 says, " But Christ being come an high priest of good things to come, by a greater and more perfect tabernacle, not made with hands, that is to say, not of this building; Neither by the blood of goats and calves, but by his own blood he entered in once into the holy place, having obtained eternal redemption for us. For if the blood of bulls and of goats, and the ashes of an heifer sprinkling the unclean, sanctifieth to the purifying of the flesh: How much more shall the blood of Christ, who through the eternal Spirit offered himself without spot to God, purge your conscience from dead works to serve the living God?"

The blood of bulls could never take away our sins. God imputed our sins to the account of Christ, one who knew no sin.

1 John 1:7 says, "...the blood of Jesus Christ his Son cleanseth us from all sin."

Because of Jesus, we do not have to live in memories of the past. We do not have to carry a load of guilt and shame. We are forgiven.

A prison chaplain shared an illustration that God used to save a soul and transform a life. The chaplain said to a prisoner, "God has a check made out to "Forgiven" and has signed it. You need to endorse the check and you will be forgiven of your sins. The prisoner went back to his cell, and in the middle of the night, he awoke and endorsed that check of his forgiveness. He was released and preaches the gospel of forgiveness today. He has witnessed hundreds endorse that check signed by God. He was ...

FORGIVEN

LEARN FROM GOD

Record one thing you learned.

LEAN ON GOD

Remember to pray. Offer a prayer of thanks to God for his forgiveness and ask Him to help you forgive others.

LAUGH WITH GOD

Read and share.

One man in the choir could not sing a note in tune even if his life depended on it. Several people hinted to him that he would make an excellent usher, but he continued to go to choir practice. The choir director and some members of the choir became desperate and pleaded with the pastor. "You've got to get that man out of the choir," they begged. "If you don't, our Christmas cantata will be ruined, and the other choir members will quit. Please do something!" So, the pastor when to the man and suggested, "Perhaps you should leave the choir." "Why should I quit the choir?" he asked. "Well, I hate to say this because I have no ear for music, but five or six people have told me that you can't sing." "That's nothing," the man snorted, "Twenty-five people have told me that you can't preach!"

Day 3

LISTEN TO GOD

Read Psalms 3, 33, 63, 93, and 123

SLEEP WELL

"I laid me down and slept. I awakened, for the Lord sustained me." Psalm 3:5

For years, parents have used a prayer to help put their children to sleep at night: "Now I lay me down to sleep, I pray the Lord my soul to keep. If I should die before I wake, I pray the Lord my soul to take." The origin of this prayer is in debate. Some say it first appeared in an essay by Joseph Addison printed in *The Spectator* on March 8, 1711: "When I lay me down to sleep, I recommend myself to his care. When I awake, I give myself up to His Direction." Some say the prayer originated from an old English prayer by Thomas Fleet that was printed in the New England Primer in 1737: "Matthew, Mark, Luke, and John, bless the bed that I lie on. Four angels round my head, one to watch, one to pray, and two to bear my soul away. Now I lay me down to sleep, I pray the Lord my soul to keep. If I should die before I wake, I pray the lord my soul to take." It is said that President John Adams said this prayer every night before he went to sleep.

According to the Center of Disease Control and Prevention, 35% of adults in America aren't getting enough sleep. Stress is the most common cause of chronic insomnia. Doctors have prescribed numerous drugs to aid in sleep.

When my wife and I started our family, we would tuck our children in their beds in their own rooms. The next morning, one or sometimes both of them would be in our bed. When the exchange took place, I never knew. They would awake in the night and for security, get in the bed with Mommy and Daddy.

From birth to age nine, I slept in the same room with my parents. They had their bed, and I had mine. Mine was an old roll-away bed. It was no more than ten feet from their bed. On some real stormy, scary nights, they would pull my bed up next to theirs to help me sleep. What psychological damage that did to me is debatable. But I still remember I slept well when I was near Mommy and Daddy. I believe to this day that we sleep well when near our heavenly Father.

Philippians 4:6-7 says, "Be careful for nothing; but in every thing by prayer and supplication with thanksgiving let your requests be made known unto God. And the peace of God, which passeth all understanding, shall keep your hearts and minds through Christ Jesus."

Believe this and ...

SLEEP WELL

LEARN FROM GOD

Record one thing you learned.

LEAN ON GOD

Remember to pray. Pray before you go to sleep each night, taking your concerns to God and offering thanks for his provision and his peace.

LAUGH WITH GOD

Read and share.

Have you ever been guilty of looking at others your own age and thinking that you surely can't be that old? Well, listen to this one.

My name is Alice, and I was sitting in the waiting room for my first appointment with a new dentist. I noticed his DDS diploma, which bore his full name, on the wall. Suddenly, I remembered a tall, handsome, dark-haired boy with the same name that had been in my high school class some 30-plus years ago.

Could he be the same guy I had a secret crush on, way back then?

Upon seeing him, however, I quickly discarded any such thought. This balding, gray-haired man with the deeply lined face was way too old to have been my classmate.

After he examined my teeth, I asked him if he had attended Morgan Park High School. "Yes. Yes, I did. I'm a Mustang," he stated with pride.

"When did you graduate?" I asked.

He answered, "In 1980. Why do you ask?"

I exclaimed, "You were in my class!"

He looked at me closely. Then, that ugly, old, bald, wrinkled-faced, gray-haired, decrepit, old man asked, "What did you teach?"

Day 4

LISTEN TO GOD

Read Psalms 4, 34, 64, 94, and 124.

PRAYER

Psalm 4:1, "Hear me when I call, O God of my righteousness: thou hast enlarged me when I was in distress; have mercy upon me, and hear my prayer."

Psalm 34:4, "I sought the Lord, and he heard me, and delivered me from all my fears."

Psalm 64:1, "Hear my voice, O God, in my prayer: preserve my life from fear of the enemy."

Psalm 94:19, "In the multitude of my thoughts within me thy comforts delight my soul."

Psalm 124:8, "Our help is in the name of the Lord, who made heaven and earth."

Prayer is the greatest privilege; lack of prayer is the Christian's greatest problem. Prayer is so refreshing, but prayer is also work. Prayers are known by God before we ask, and yet prayers go unanswered because we do not ask. Prayer has been one of the most difficult disciplines of my Christian walk. I have never been satisfied. I have tried different times, from early morning to noon break, to right before I retire at night. I have tried various formulas, such as the following:

P – PRAISE
R – REMEMBER THANKSGIVING
A – ADMIT YOUR SINS
Y – YOURSELF AND OTHERS
A – ADORATION
C – CONFESSION
T – THANKSGIVING
S – SUPPLICATION

There are over 650 different prayers in the Bible. Prayer, our most untapped resource, has been defined as simply talking to God. F.B. Meyer said, "The great tragedy of life is not unanswered prayer, but unoffered prayer."

I have read about, been told about, and personally experienced the power of prayer many times. My seminary professor told of how a wife prayed for fifty years for her husband to come to salvation. On their fiftieth wedding anniversary, he came to church because that's all she wanted as a gift from him. He heard the gospel and was saved.

I served as pastor at a church that had a bus ministry. The bus captain said that all who came to church for four Sundays would get a kite. Then he said that everyone who brought his or her parents on the last Sunday would get a string with the kite. The children all prayed that their parents would come to church. Kay and James Dennis came to church for the first time on that last Sunday and were saved. Kay became a great Sunday School teacher and James became a deacon.

Numerous times I have prayed with people who had the dreaded "C Word", cancer. I learned later that they were healed. In my time as a college president, I have had to trust God several times when the college would be out of funds at the end of a semester. Many on staff would pray. At the last hour, a check would come. God provided.

There is much written on prayer. My closing advice would be to pray with persistence. Pray daily. Pray when you don't feel like it. Pray when driving down the highway. Pray while lying in bed. Pray in a designated place. Pray publicly. Pray privately. In Luke 11 and 18, Jesus taught parables about the value of being persistent.

Just pray. Don't analyze it.

JUST PRAY

LEARN FROM GOD

Record one thing you learned.

LEAN ON GOD

Remember to pray. Pray with persistence, trusting in God to hear and answer you.

LAUGH WITH GOD

Read and share.

Why does Ms. Jones have a problem remembering passwords? Because her password is:

Mickey, Minnie, Pluto, Huey, Louie, Dewey, Donald, Goofy.

When asked the reason for such a long password, she answered, "Mr. Smith said it had to be at least eight characters long."

Day 5

LISTEN TO GOD

Read Psalms 5 35, 65, 95, and 125.

WORSHIP

Psalm 95 is part of the psalms which the Israelites would sing as they went to worship. It is in the midst of the group of praise and worship psalms, Psalms 93 through 100. Psalm 95 makes two appeals in worship.

Psalm 95:1, ": O come, let us sing unto the LORD: let us make a joyful noise to the rock of our salvation."

Psalm 95:6, "O come, let us worship and bow down: let us kneel before the LORD our maker."

In this psalm, the two appeals for worship are to sing and to pray.

I am the last person you should consult for instruction when it comes to singing. I am tone deaf. In the fourth grade, I was asked to leave the choir and help the teacher erase the blackboards while my classmates sang. At church, the youth choir leaders asked if I would sit in the bus and guard it while the choir went in to sing. My wife has jabbed me in my ribs on more than one occasion, her way of indicating to me that I was not to sing even though the church's music director had just instructed us to stand and sing. According to her, these instructions did not apply to me.

I not only have a complex about singing, but also have an awareness that singing is one area about which I am least qualified to speak. However, I have strong opinions on the subject. I may not know the technical aspect of music, but I know what I like and don't like.

I have watched music in church change over the last fifty years. Organs and pianos have been replaced with keyboards, drums, and loud bass guitars. Choirs have often been replaced with praise teams. Choir robes have given way to t-shirts and jeans and hymn books have become words on a screen. Hymns have been replaced with praise songs that my mother-in-law called "little ditties." A friend called such hymns "7-11" songs – 7 words sung 11 times.

Worship wars, or wars over the style of music, are still one of the top ten causes of church conflict. I am not saying that all the changes I mentioned are evil. The autonomous church has the right to select it's preferred style of music. Regardless of the music style, my desire is that the congregation engage in worship.

Jesus said that His house is to be a house of prayer. There may be three prayers in the average worship service. I have attended some that may only have one. My intent is not to be critical or cause conflict but rather to cry out to church leaders and encourage them to actively lead their congregations in worship.

Singing and praying are two powerful forces. They should be a priority in public and private

WORSHIP

LEARN OF GOD

Record on thing you learned.

LEAN ON GOD

Remember to pray. Pray that you will learn to make worship a priority in your life.

LAUGH WITH GOD

Read and share.

A four-year old girl often forgot to close the door when coming in from outside. Finally, her father scolder her, "Shut that door! Were you born in a barn?" She looked at her father and replied softly, "No, but Jesus was."

Day 6

LISTEN TO GOD

Read Psalms 6, 36, 66, 96, and 126.

SOULS

Psalm 126:1-6, "When the LORD turned again the captivity of Zion, we were like them that dream. Then was our mouth filled with laughter, and our tongue with singing: then said they among the heathen, The LORD hath done great things for them. The LORD hath done great things for us; whereof we are glad. Turn again our captivity, O LORD, as the streams in the south. They that sow in tears shall reap in joy. He that goeth forth and weepeth, bearing precious seed, shall doubtless come again with rejoicing, bringing his sheaves with him."

This psalm was probably written by Ezra on the return from Babylon. The Hebrews had been in captivity, separated from their homeland and enslaved in a stressful existence. While in Babylon, they hung their harps on the willows and shed tears of lament.

Now, there was laughter. They were dancing in the sweetness of their return. They learned the truth that those who sow in tears will reap in joy.

Pain and suffering, whether physical, emotional, or spiritual, will drive us away from God or closer to God. God had sent the Israelites into captivity as gold ore is put into the fire to remove the dross. We, at times, must suffer in order to see and experience the hand of God. The lost and unchurched around us watch how we followers of Christ respond in times of suffering. The truth of this psalm is that in life, we will have times of suffering and shedding of tears. God hears and brings joy.

However, I want to concentrate on Verse 6 in a devotional way as we close. "He that goeth forth and weepeth, bearing precious seed, shall doubtless come again with rejoicing, bringing his sheaves with him." Two things are mentioned in this verse that I see little of in most churches: tears and soul winning. We all want to laugh, to have a good time, to experience joy, to see our church grow. Yet are we willing to pay the price?

Who are you shedding tears for today? Do you have a family member or a friend who would, as far as you know, spend eternity in hell if he or she died today? This should move us to tears. Every invitation in a church should witness God's people at the altar crying for the lost.

In days gone by, I've seen mothers, with tears streaming down their cheeks, at the altar, praying for their wayward sons. I've seen wives at the altar begging God to save their lost husbands. One such wife asked me to go visit her husband. I scheduled an appointment. He was cordial and friendly as I entered. We swapped small talk of weather and the Dallas Cowboys. Then I took my Bible and asked, "Can I share with you how to be saved?" He literally leaped out of his chair across the room and knelt on his knees beside me. He said that he was ready. He was saved that night. His salvation was not the result of my witness, but the result of the tears and prayers of a concerned wife.

Though sowing precious seeds through sharing the gospel, sharing our testimony of salvation, or sharing the Roman Road, should be our hearts desire, there is a real lack of Christians sowing seeds. Yet, the principle is clear. First come the tears, next the sowing, and then the joy of ...

SOULS

LEARN FROM GOD

Record one thing you learned.

LEAN ON GOD

Remember to pray. Pray for your family and friends who are lost and pray for the courage to share the Gospel.

LAUGH WITH GOD

Read and share.

The little boy wasn't getting good marks in school. One day he made the teacher quite surprised. He tapped her on the shoulder and said, "I don't want to scare you, but my daddy says if I don't get better grades, somebody is going to get a spanking."

Day 7

LISTEN TO GOD

Read Psalms 7, 37, 67, 97, and 127.

EVIL

I was in the fifth grade, living in a new town, in a new home, and starting in a new school again. My dad was an oilfield roughneck, so we moved from one oilfield town to the next boom town. I never attended the same school for more than two years in a row. Kids will be kids, but the treatment received for being a new kid is difficult. The name calling and the shunning inflicts real emotional harm. After fifty-plus years since that day, I wish I could report that it was just kid's stuff. But no: on jobs, in churches, in neighborhoods, evildoers exist at every age of life.

David, In Psalm 37, gives us some encouraging and instructional words on how to respond to evildoers. I have read them often.

- v. 1 – Fret not yourself because of evildoers.
- v. 3 – Trust in the Lord.
- v. 4 – Delight yourself in the Lord.

- v. 5 – Commit thy way unto the Lord.
- v. 7 – Rest in the Lord, wait patiently for Him.
- v. 8 – Cease from anger.
- v. 9 – For evildoers shall be cut off.
- v. 10 – For yet a little while and wicked shall not be.
- v. 23 – The steps of a good man are ordered by the Lord.
- v. 25 – I have been young, and now I am old; yet, I have not seen the righteous forsaken nor his seed begging for bread.
- v. 34 – Wait on the Lord.
- v. 36 – The salvation of the righteous is of the Lord.
- v. 40 – And the Lord shall help them and deliver them: He shall deliver them from the wicked, and save them, because they trust in Him.

Sometimes evildoers attack, and when they do, our only recourse is to read God's Word and wait on Him. He will protect us from ...

EVIL

LEARN FROM GOD

Record one thing you learned.

LEAN ON GOD

Lord, I need help in my attitude toward those who seek to harm me. Lord, protect me from evil doers for your name sake.

LAUGH WITH GOD

Read and share.

A young preacher was being interviewed by his first pulpit committee when the chairman asked, "Young man, do you know your Bible?"

He replied, "I think I know it pretty good."

So, the chairman said, "Well, what part do you know the best?"

And he said, "I guess I know the New Testament the best."

Then the chairman said, "Why don't you tell us a story from the New Testament. Why don't you tell us the story about the prodigal son?"

So, the young preacher said, "Okay," swallowed, pulled his collar and told this story.

"There was a man of the Pharisees named Nicodemus who went down to Jericho by night. And he fell upon stony ground, and the thorns choked him half to death. The next day, when Solomon and his wife Gomorrah came by, they carried him down to the ark so Moses could take care of him. But while entering the ark through the eastern gate, he caught his hair in the limb of a tree, and he hung there for forty days and forty nights. And afterward, when he hungered, the ravens came and fed him. When he recovered, the wise men took him down to the boat dock where he caught a ship bound for Nineveh. When he got there, he saw Delilah sitting on the wall and he said, "Cast her down, boys." And they said, "How many times shall we cast her down? Til seven times seven?"

But he said, "Nay, but seventy times seven." So, they cast her down four hundred ninety times, and she burst asunder in their midst. And of the fragments, they picked up twelve baskets full. And in the resurrection, whose wife will she be?"

The chairman looked at the other members of the committee and said, "Well, fellas, I think we ought to call him. He's awfully young, but he really knows his Bible."

Day 8

LISTEN TO GOD

Read Psalms 8, 38, 68, 98, and 128.

CREATOR

Psalm 8 is a classic psalm of praise. Reread it and let it soak in.

Our God is the God of the universe. He is the Creator of the heavens, earth, and man. Sit back and look at the sun, moon, stars, lakes, and mountains and stand in awe. God made this. He spoke it into existence.

The earth is 92.96 million miles away from the sun. The point in its orbit at which the earth is closest to the sun is called perihelion. This occurs in early January, when the earth is about 91 million miles away from the sun. The point at which the earth is farthest away from the sun is called aphelion. This comes in early July, when the distance from the earth to the sun is about 94.5 million miles.

The earth makes a complete revolution around the sun every 365.5 days. The earth's axis is tilted 23.5 degrees. This tilt is what gives us our seasons. In this circular orbit the earth is traveling at a speed of 67,000 miles per hour. The sun's temperature is 27 million degrees Fahrenheit.

Why are these exact figures important? Consider this. The earth's distance from the sun is just right. If Earth were any closer to the sun, we would burn up. If Earth were any farther from the sun, we would freeze. Earth's speed around the sun is just right. If Earth traveled any faster, it could sling us into space. If Earth traveled any slower, we could freeze. Earth's tilt is just right. If Earth were tilted any closer to the sun, we would burn up. If Earth tilted any farther away from the sun, we could all freeze to death.

Now you can believe in evolution, which is a theory. The fact is that we have never had one species that evolved into another species. Yes, we have seen evolution within a species, but a horse has never evolved into a cat. Yes, you can believe in the Big Bang Theory, which says that particles of space banged into one another to create the earth. That's like believing that a tornado could hit a junkyard and somehow end up making a Boeing 747.

For me, it is much easier to believe that "In the beginning, God created the heavens and the earth." Genesis 1:1. For me, I will praise His name. Oh God, our Lord, how excellent is Your name. God is ...

CREATOR

LEARN FROM GOD

Record one thing you learned today.

LEAN ON GOD

Lord, I acknowledge you are creator. You are God and beside you there is none other.

LAUGH WITH GOD

In the tall grass of an unkempt cemetery, a headstone was found with the following engraved:

"Pause, stranger, when you pass me by,

For as you are, so once was I.

As I am now, so you will be.

Then prepare unto death and follow me."

Crudely scratched below the verse someone added:

"To follow you I'm not content

Until I know which way you went"

Day 9

LISTEN TO GOD

Read Psalms 9, 39, 69, 99, and 129

NATIONS

The wicked shall be turned into hell, and all the nations that forget God" (Psalm 9:17)

More than one preacher has said that God has two hands: a hand of grace and a hand of justice. His hand of grace gives us what we do not deserve. We are saved by grace, according to Ephesians 2:8-10. God's hand of justice thrusts the unbeliever into hell. Hell is real. It is a place of endless torment and suffering. To me, what makes hell the ultimate torment is the eternal suffering from God. All people in history who have rejected Jesus as Savior, regardless of how good or kind they have appeared to be to others, will go to hell. Every church member who had his or her name on a church roll but never had room in his or her heart for Jesus will go to hell. Every person who left Jesus out of his or her life but meant to start following Him and just never found the time will go to hell. The wicked shall be turned into hell.

Psalm 9:17 is a solemn verse. How can anyone forget God? This verse serves as a reminder that even moral, honest, kind "good ole boys who will give you the shirt off their back, who stand for the national anthem and who die for their country" can forget God. They let life slip by and never commit to follow Him. They acknowledge God in their heads, but eighteen inches away, they have no room in their hearts. This is who about whom old preachers used to say, "Most people miss heaven by eighteen inches." They mentally consent to the existence of a god, but they never have room in their hearts for him. A person who has no room for God in his or her heart, head, and vocabulary, forgets God.

Apparently, individuals are not the only ones who can forget God. In some cases, a whole nation seems to forget God. These nations do not acknowledge Him and they even pass laws to exclude His name or His words from public places. They can focus on other priorities and deny God's existence. America was founded by people who sought religious freedom. America's laws were patterned after the Ten Commandments. As a whole and in general, nations that forget God give themselves over to idolatry and sin. Unfortunately, America as a nation has drifted away from God. There are those under the influence of Satan who try to rid our nation of any acknowledgment of God. More than once, I have read of both a college professor and a high school teacher who warned their classes that if someone sneezed, they did not want to hear anyone reply, "God bless you," because it would cause a distraction for the class. The Bible is clear that there is coming a day of judgment of nations who forget God. Just as there will be individuals in hell, there will be nations destroyed.

Matthew 25 speaks of a judgment of nations. The nations will be judged on how they treated Israel. Some apply this to how a Christian respond to those in need. The application is permissible, but the interpretation is clear that there will be a judgment of nations. The judgment is not to be confused with the Judgment Seat of Christ or the Great White Throne of judgment. The Judgment Seat of Christ is only for Christians, according to 2 Corinthians 5. The Great White Throne of Judgment is only for lost people, according to Revelation 20:11-14. The judgment of nations is based on how nations have treated Israel. That is why I am pro-Israel. If Israel asks America for forty planes, I say we sell them the planes in order to help them. The Bible is clear that whoever is a friend of Israel is a friend of God.

Genesis 12:3 says, "And I will bless them that bless thee, and curse him that curseth thee: and in thee shall all families of the earth be blessed."

2 Samuel 7:23-24 says, "And what one nation in the earth is like thy people, even like Israel, whom God went to redeem for a people to himself, and to make him a name, and to do for you great things and terrible, for thy land, before thy people, which thou redeemedst to thee from Egypt, from the nations and their gods? For thou hast confirmed to thyself thy people Israel to be a people unto thee for ever: and thou, LORD, art become their God."

There is little doubt that Israel is a special ...

NATION

LEARN FROM GOD

Record one thing you learned.

LEAN ON GOD

Lord, I pray for America. Please give her a Revival. Lord, I pray for Israel.

LAUGH WITH GOD

Read and share.

A lady missionary received a letter from home with a ten-dollar bill inside. Looking out her window, she saw a shabbily dressed man below. She put the ten-dollar bill in an envelope, wrote "Don't despair" on the outside, and threw it down to him. He picked it up, opened it, looked up at her, smiled, and tipped his hat. The next day, he knocked on the door. When she opened it, he handed her sixty dollars. When she asked what the money was for, he replied, "That's the money you won, lady. 'Don't Despair' paid five to one."

Day 10

LISTEN TO GOD

Read Psalms 10, 40, 70, 100, and 130.

THE PITS

Are you in a pit? Are you having the pits? What is the pits? A pit could be emotional distress; sorrow over the loss of a spouse is the pits. Your pit could be financial stress; debt is the pits. Your pit could be an enemy; being betrayed or lied to is the pits. Your pit could be the loss of a job. "You're fired" is the pits. Psalm 40 is a song about the pits. Psalm 40:1-10 tells how David gets out of the pits, and Psalm 40:11-17 described David in another pit. So, I am not going to promise you that once you get out of a pit you will not experience another pit. No, truthfully you will be in and out of numerous pits all your life. But let's focus on some biblical insight into Psalm 40:1-10 to learn how to get out of the pits.

- **Wait on the Lord** (Psalm 40:1). Waiting on the Lord is a common theme in Scripture. For the most part, when we hear the word *wait*, we picture inactivity. *Wait* here in the Hebrew does not mean passively waiting like we experience in a doctor's office as we thumb through countless out-of-date magazines. *Wait* in Psalm 40:1 is an intensified form of a verb. This intensified form means to be active in your pit, with the hope that God is working to help you out.

We are in a hurry and often get frustrated when we are in a pit and God does not instantly rescue us. David said when he was in the pit he cried out to God, "O Lord, make haste to help me" (Psalm 40:13). Prayer is a very passionate activity. Prayer is not to be our last resort in a pit but our first resource to get out of the pit. Numerous times, I have been in an emotional pit. I started praying, and by the end of the prayer, I was out of the pit. Oftentimes when we are in a pit, we think we can get ourselves out. We waste time struggling, slipping and sliding, and get mud all over us. If we would just wait on God in prayer, He would deliver us out of the pit.

- **Worship the Lord** (Psalm 40:3). Worship is focusing in on God. Two activities associated with worship are praying and singing. But worship can be giving or listening.

When you are in the pit, sing Psalm 100.

But what if you do not feel like praying when you are in the pit? Pray regardless of your feelings. But what if you do not feel like praising the Lord when you are in the pit? Praise God regardless of the pit. Worship God in the pit and worship God out of the pit. Do what is right. Wait on God, worship God, and pray.

Do this and you might get out of ...

THE PITS

LEARN OF GOD

Record one thing you learned.

LEAN ON GOD

Lord, I have been in the pits and you restored unto me joy. I pray for friends today who are in the pits.

LAUGH WITH GOD

Read and share.

During the children's sermon, the pastor asked, "What has gray fur, eats nuts, and lives in trees?" One boy said, "I know the answer is supposed to be Jesus, but it sounds like a squirrel to me."

Day 11

LISTEN TO GOD

Read Psalms 11, 41, 71, 101, and 131.

THE FOUNDATIONS

If the foundations be destroyed, what can the righteous do?" (Psalm 11:3).

The Fugitive was a popular television series in 1963-1967. The story was about a physician who was falsely convicted of his wife's murder. On route to death row, the train he was traveling on derailed, and he escaped. Each weekly episode followed Dr. Richard Kimble on the run, being pursued by a relentless police officer by the name of Lieutenant Philip Gerard.

Psalm 11 is about David, the future King of Israel, on the run. He is being pursued by King Saul. David has been on the run for about three years. Psalm 11, like most psalms, reveals the struggles of life. This is probably why the psalms are popular. They speak to us where we walk daily. The psalm can be divided or outlined as follows:

Psalm 11:1-3 Asks Questions
Psalm 11:4-7 Answers Questions

The question we will consider today is in verse 3, "if the foundations be destroyed, what can the righteous do?"

Struggles, crises, hard times, problems all make us question. What are some of the foundations that are being destroyed?

Individual

A continuous assessment of mental health issues reveals a growing alarm. One in five adults in the United States have mental health issues. That amounts to 44 million people. Three percent of adults have bipolar disorder. Sixteen million had at least one major depression episode in the past year. Sometimes I wonder if my wife, Susan, and I are the only sane people? At times I question her. (I'm just kidding.) An observation seems to reveal that normal, hard-working, rational people are decreasing each year

Family

According to the American Psychological Association, 50% of all marriages still end in divorce. 50% of first marriages, 67% of second marriages, and 73% of third marriages end in divorce.

Church-Denomination

Thom Rainer of Lifeway Resources says between 8,000-10,000 churches close their doors every year. Church attendance has been on a decline for the last thirty years. Some say we live in a post-denomination era, a post Christian era. Another area that supports this is the baptism rate, which has fallen. William Thornton, July 20, 2016, reported baptisms dropped to 54,762 from 190,957 in 2014, hitting its lowest level in Southern Baptist churches since 1969.

Government

When David wrote this psalm, he was probably hiding in a cave. Israel's government was collapsing around King Saul.

The United States of America is the best country in the world to me. I am a patriot, but I believe the swamp needs draining. Both Republicans and Democrats seem to be ineffective in dealing with real issues. Faith in government and the president are at an all-time low.

So, what is the answer? What are we to do when the foundations are being destroyed?

Remember God is still on His throne. Psalm 11:4, "The LORD is in his holy temple, the LORD's throne is in heaven: his eyes behold, his eyelids try, the children of men."

Everything around us may be collapsing, but God is where He has always been. Changes are occurring all around us and causing chaos and confusion. Remember, God changes not. He is the same yesterday, today and tomorrow.

Follow Psalm 11:7 and keep on doing the right thing. Sometimes the world may appear as if it is going to hell in a handbasket. However, if you are a Christian, you know to do the right thing, even when all others are doing wrong. David's men wanted him to keep running, but it seems he was ready to stand. The lyrics to *"In Christ Alone"* by Keith Getty and Stuart Townend say:

> *"In Christ alone my hope is found;*
>
> *He is my light, my strength, my song;*
>
> *This cornerstone, this solid ground,*
>
> *Firm through the fiercest drought and storm,*
>
> *What heights of love, what depths of peace,*
>
> *When fears are stilled, when strivings cease!*

Dr. Mike Smith

My comforter, my all in all—

Here in the love of Christ I stand.

THE FOUNDATIONS

LEARN OF GOD

Record one thing you learned.

LEAN ON GOD

Lord, when all else around seems to be crumbling, I thank you that you are my rock and fortress. On you do I stand.

LAUGH WITH GOD

Read and share.

A young woman, going off to college, was asked by her pastor, "Are you going to work on your MRS degree?" She said she was claiming as her verse, Romans 1:13, "I would not have you ignorant brethren..."

When she came home for the Christmas break, he asked her if she was still claiming her Scripture verse. She replied that she was but that she also had a new verse. When he inquired what it was, she said it was Matthew 16:24, "If any man would come after me, let him..."

Day 12

LISTEN TO GOD

Read Psalms 12, 42, 72, 102, and 132.

DEPRESSION

Depression is a mood disorder. The symptoms affect how you feel, think, sleep, eat and work. According to the National Institute for Mental Health there are several types of depression:

- **Major Depression:** People with this type of depression experience disruptive symptoms for most of the day, every day for at least two weeks.

- **Prenatal Depression:** Women with prenatal depression experience debilitating symptoms during pregnancy or after delivery.

- **Seasonal Affective Disorder (SAD):** SAD is a type of depression that comes and goes with the seasons.

- **Psychotic Depression:** This disorder can cause hallucinations and other psychotic disorders.

- **Manic-Depression or Bipolar:** This disorder causes extreme mood swings that alternate between emotional highs and lows.

Depression can be caused by a combination of genetic, biological, environmental, and psychological factors. Depression can happen at any age, and it affects different people in different ways. Treatments can vary from counseling, medications, and/or brain stimulation. There is help for depression.

Some help for depression:

- Stop Looking at Yourself. Psalms 42 and 43 use "I" 14 times and "me" 16 times and "my" 21 times.
- Stop Looking at Your Past.

Two extreme trends in America today are a fascination with the future and a growing market for the past, ancestry, and nostalgia. There is a right and wrong use of both. In thinking about the past, be sure to include God. Psalm 42:6, "O my God, my soul is cast down within me: therefore will I remember thee from the land of Jordan..."

- Start Standing on the Promises. When you are cast down and depressed, seek God and stand on His promises. Psalm 42:8 says, "Yet the LORD will command his lovingkindness in the day time, and in the night his song shall be with me, and my prayer unto the God of my life." Verse 11 adds, "...hope thou in God..."

DEPRESSION

LEARN OF GOD

Record one thing you learned.

LEAN ON GOD

Lord, help me to see you and not focus on myself.

LAUGH WITH GOD

Read and share.

A teacher asked the children in her Sunday School class, "If I sold all I own and had a big garage sale and gave all my money to the church, would I get into heaven?"

"NO!" all the children answered.

"If I cleaned the church every day, took care of the yard, and kept everything neat and orderly, would I get into heaven?"

"NO!" they answered again.

"Well then, how can I get to heaven?"

One serious boy said, "You gotta be dead!"

Day 13

LISTEN TO GOD

Read Psalms 13, 43, 73, 103, and 133.

UNITY

Albert Garner, in his book *Pearls in the Psalms,* defines unity as "diversity living in harmony." We live in a world that values diversity and devalues unity. Some refer to this present generation as the "me generation", as if to say, "Life is all about me."

Psalm 133 is one of David's fifteen psalms of ascents or degrees (Psalms 120-134). The belief held by many is that these psalms were sung by worshippers as they ascended the road to Jerusalem. Others think they were sung by Levites as they ascended the fifteen steps to serve in the temple. (Wikipedia.org).

David was the one who united the twelve tribes of Israel. He led a divided nation that was suspicious of each other and was an open target for surrounding enemy nations who could unite against them. David planned the temple to be a symbol of spiritual unity.

1. **David Declares the Value of Unity:** "Behold, how good and how pleasant it is for brethren to dwell

together in unity!" (Psalm 133:1). Unity is what Jesus prayed for in John 17:21: "...that they all may be one." Love for one another is one of the evidences God gives that we are Christians: "We know that we have passed from death unto life, because we love the brethren. He that loveth not his brother abideth in death" (1 John 3:14). Acts 2:44 describes the unity of the first church after Pentecost: "And all that believed were together, and had all things common;"

Unity does not mean conformity. God has made all of us unique and with different personalities, different talents, and different spiritual gifts. Unity is brought about by the work of God. The common element believers have is the indwelling of the Holy Spirit. When believers act in maturity, are led by the Spirit, and obey the Word of God, you will see unity. Men attempt to create unity. The coach of a sports team demands, "We play as a team." Organizations create charts to visualize the unity of their organization and how everyone relates to one another.

What is unity? David gives two illustrations:

2. **David Describes Unity:** " It is like the precious ointment upon the head, that ran down upon the beard, even Aaron's beard: that went down to the skirts of his garments; As the dew of Hermon, and as the dew that descended upon the mountains of Zion: for there the LORD commanded the blessing, even life for evermore" (Psalm 133:2-3).

   a. Oil (v. 2)

   The oil was made of myrrh, sweet cinnamon, and a blend of various oils with olive oil. Aaron, the priest, before entering the Holy of Holies, was to wash, put on clean garments, and put on the oil that gave a sweet odor. Oil is a symbol of the Holy Spirit. We cannot come into the Presence of God until we repent of our sins, cleansed by the blood of Jesus, and have the Holy Spirit within.

    b.   Dew (v. 3)

        Dew forms only when all is still and at rest and never in or after a storm. In the hot climate of Israel, dew was vital to plant life. Dew could not be created by man but is a gift from God. Dew is a symbol of unity. Just as physical dew comes when all is at rest and never in a storm, spiritual unity comes when believers live in peace with one another.

3. **David Directs Us to Unity:** "for there the LORD commanded the blessing, even life for evermore" (Psalm 133:3b). God does not want a church in conflict. I've been part of over 3,000 church conflicts as a consultant. Churches have literally split over the color of the carpet, but more often the split is over who controls the church. Usually after a church split, it takes 10 years to recover. The witness and effectiveness of the church is hampered. A church in conflict quenches the Spirit. A church that God blesses is a church in ...

UNITY

LEARN OF GOD

Record one thing you learned.

LEAN ON GOD

Lord, you prayed for the unity of your people and I pray for unity today.

LAUGH WITH GOD

Read and share.

A man was marooned on a deserted island for several years. Finally, a passing ship saw the smoke from his rescue fire and sent a boat with several sailors to rescue him. Overjoyed to finally be getting off the island, he asked if he could collect his things before they left. They agreed and offered to help. Following the man to a clearing, they saw three huts. Asked what these were, the man said the first hut was where he lived and the third was where he went to church. When asked what the second hut was, he said it was where he had attended church until he felt offended.

Day 14

LISTEN TO GOD

Read Psalms 14, 44, 74, 104, and 134.

WHO, WHAT, WHEN, WHERE, WHY?

Anyone who enrolls in my Old Testament and New Testament survey courses will be required to know five things about every book in the Bible. I am of the conviction that biblical literacy is at an all-time low. Stand in front of a college classroom or a local church and instruct those in attendance to number their paper from one to sixty-six and write all of the books of the Bible in order and to spell them correctly. You will be surprised, or more likely, disappointed. So often students of the Bible want to know where Cain got his wife or when Jesus is coming back. They attempt to study the Bible without the foundation. One must have a solid, simple foundation of the Bible or the result could be a faulty interpretation.

So, we are going to look in Psalm 134 at the foundational questions of who, what, when, where, and why.

Who?

Who wrote this psalm? Who is the subject of this Psalm?

Psalm 134 is a song that was sung by those traveling to Jerusalem to the temple to worship. So, this would be one that we would subscribe to David as the author.

In Psalm 130, he sang of the pardon of the Lord.
In Psalm 131, he sang of the patience of the Lord.
In Psalm 132, he sang of the promise of the Lord.
In Psalm 133, he sang of the people of the Lord.
In Psalm 134, he sang of the power of the Lord.

The subject of Psalm 134 is the servant of the Lord - - you. Look at Psalm 134:1, "...bless ye the LORD, all ye servants of the LORD..." I do not consider myself to be gifted in music, yet this psalm says I am to sing. I do sing. My best singing is in my truck with my only audience being God.

What?

What type of literature is the psalm?

It is a psalm, part of the five Wisdom Books. It is the last of the Songs of Degrees (Psalms 120-134). These were songs worshippers sang as they made their way to the temple.

What does this passage tell us to do?

"Lift up your hands in the sanctuary..." (Psalm 134:2). This was or is a symbolic act. Many interpretations can be drawn from this act. One is that we are emptying ourselves of self and asking God to set us aside and use us, fill us with His Holy Spirit.

When?

"...which by night stand in the house of the Lord" (Psalm 134:1b). Two thoughts here: If David is the author, it was written towards the end of his life in 1015 B.C. If Ezra wrote it, then he wrote it on the return from captivity in 536 B.C.

Where?

"Behold, bless ye the Lord, all ye servants of the Lord, which by night stand in the house of the Lord. Lift up your hands in the sanctuary, and bless the Lord" (Psalm 134:1-2). The place of worship in the Old Testament was the tabernacle in the wilderness, the temple in Jerusalem, and the synagogue in the captivity or Diaspora. The New Testament clearly reveals that the Holy Spirit lives within every believer, and a believer can worship God anywhere, anytime. Yet the New Testament is clear that we are not to forsake the assembling of ourselves together. We are to worship as a church, the body of Christ in local places, be it under a bridge, in a storefront, or in a stained-glass edifice.

Why?

" The LORD that made heaven and earth bless thee out of Zion" (Psalm 134:3).

God is our Creator and deserves our praises. God is the author of our salvation and deserves our praise.

I have had the privilege of worshipping in all types of places, such as under a bridge with homeless people, in a tent beside a burned down church building, under a tree in Africa, in a storefront, in a public school, in a prison behind locked doors, in marvelous architectural building in Europe, in houses in China, in hotel rooms, in multimillion-dollar buildings in America. I've sung all types of music, including hymns, gospel songs, choruses, and country and western music. Some have been slow, some lively, and some so loud I couldn't hear myself sing. I've sung with all types of people, some cold, indifferent, and unfriendly. One met me in the parking lot, told me I was not welcome there, and not to get out of the car. I once had to have a police escort just to help get me inside to safety. Many welcomed me and were kind and friendly. But worship is not about the place, the music style, or the people. Worship is from my heart to God.

Psalm 134 reminds us of the value of worship as it answers ...

WHO, WHAT, WHEN, WHERE, WHY?

LEARN OF GOD

Record one thing you learned.

LEAN ON GOD

Lord, I worship you whenever and wherever.

LAUGH WITH GOD

Read and share.

Two businessmen went sailing, when a freak storm wrecked their boat and left them marooned on a deserted island. By the third day, one of the men was pacing constantly. The other reclined peacefully on the sand.

"Aren't you afraid we're going to die?" the first man wailed.

"Not really," his friend replied. "I make a lot of money and I give ten percent to my church. You don't need to worry. My pastor will find us."

Day 15

LISTEN TO GOD

Read Psalms 15, 45, 75, 105, and 135.

TOUCH NOT GOD'S ANOINTED

An irate person approached the pastor and began to repeatedly hit the pastor's chest with his index finger. The reason for the anger escaped me. What followed, I will never forget. That person, after the verbal and physical attack on the pastor, when home, and in an accident, the very finger he used against the pastor was cut off.

I have worked with pastors and churches in over 3,000 church conflicts. It's sad to admit that I have had several situations where a person opposed their pastor, and the result was not pleasant.

A church was in a building program. The majority were excited and committed to contribute. On the night of the vote, the pastor shared his heart in support of the project to build. When the vote was taken, it passed by a large percent, but five people opposed the building program and the leadership of the pastor. Within one year of that business meeting, the pastor preached the funerals of those five people.

I love visiting with older pastors. All my ministry, I've sought out friendships with older pastors. More than one shared how in the time from the 1930s through the 1950s, a church member who wanted to get rid of the pastor would start a "woman tale." By this they meant, the individual would say to another person, "Have you noticed how Pastor Brown visits Widow Jones every week?" Or, "I was told by a reliable source that they saw Pastor Brown with that new single woman in town out at the lake." More time than not, the gossip would spread, causing pain to the pastor and his family. He would usually resign and leave town rather than stay and fight the accusation.

Social media today has caused harm to more than one pastor. Some people freely degrade a pastor without there being any truth to what they say.

Psalm 15:3 warns that a person who slanders with his tongue, or does evil to his neighbor, will not abide in God's house.

Psalm 105:15 says, "...Touch not mine anointed, and do my prophets no harm."

There are numerous views on who God's anointed are. Some say this referring to Abraham. Some say this includes all the patriarchs. Some say it is all the prophets, priests, and kings. Some say it refers only to the nation of Israel. Some say it refers to all believers, all Christians.

There is a true sense that every believer is set apart, anointed of God from sin and self to righteousness and unto Him. But it would be hard to deny that within this full body of Christ, God calls out and sets apart those for service. I have no trouble accepting that this passage of protection applies to all believers, but it certainly could apply to pastors and preachers of the gospel.

Can a pastor be wrong? Certainly. Should a pastor every be rebuked? Certainly. However, one better be careful that the rebuke is consistent with the Bible and not out of personal emotion.

In Proverbs 6:1-19 is a list of seven things that God hates. The sixth is a false witness who speaks lies, and the seventh is one who sows discord among the brethren. Pope Gregory I, around the year 600, referred to these as the Seven Deadly Sins.

1 Peter 4:15 includes a busybody in the same list as murderers.

My heart has been broken and I have shed tears numerous times as I have listened to pastors and pastor's wives share how people have lied about them and tried to hurt them. I do not share this to lift me up, but I share this to reveal the ugliness of sin.

After a service, an angry woman approached me and swung her purse at me. She screamed, "Do not bring another one of those barefoot Mexicans in our church." Her husband and brother grabbed me and circled me, saying that if I ever brought a Mexican to church, they would see to it that I never pastored again. Shortly after, the irate woman's son was walking along the street after a windstorm and stepped on a high voltage power line and lost his foot. Remember what the woman said to the preacher? "Don't bring a barefooted Mexican into my church." Now her son has no foot on which to come to church. Remember:

TOUCH NOT GOD'S ANOINTED

LEARN OF GOD

Record one thing you learned.

LEAN ON GOD

Lord, I pray for the pastors and their families who are hurting today. Give them some joy and protect your name in their ministry.

LAUGH WITH GOD

Read and share.

One church installed sanitary hot air hand dryers in the restrooms, but after two weeks, they were removed even though they worked just fine. When asked why the dryers had been removed, the pastor said that he'd gone in the restroom and discovered a sign that read "PUSH THIS BUTTON FOR A SAMPLE OF THIS WEEK'S SERMON."

Day 16

LISTEN TO GOD

Read Psalms 16, 46, 76, 106, and 136.

PRAY

"Mike Smith, will you pray for us?" The first time I heard those words, sweat drops burst onto my forehead. I had never prayed in public. I was shy, and to be honest, I had never thought about what to say. That prayer was short and softly spoken. Sometime shortly after that experience, I came across some books on prayer. I started a quest to learn how to pray, and I came across an acronym that provided an outline for prayer.

P – Presence of God (Praise)
R – Remember God (Thanksgiving)
A – Admit my Sins to God (Confession)
Y – Yourself and Others Needs to God (Petition)

This simple outline acrostic PRAY has provided me with a structure that has built confidence in me to pray. I have been asked to pray in various settings, before small and large numbers. I've prayed with just one person. I've prayed in small Sunday School rooms of twenty. I've prayed in church worship services with five hundred people. I've prayed in denominational meetings with thousands. I've prayed at Lions Club, Rotary Club, and other civic gatherings of leaders of the community. PRAY is still the pattern I use. Today I want to draw select verses from our five psalms to expand upon the subject PRAY.

P - Presence of God (Praise)

Psalm 16:1, "Preserve me, O God: for in thee do I put my trust."

Psalm 16:8, "I have set the Lord always before me: because he is at my right hand, I shall not be moved."

Psalm 46:10, "Be still, and know that I am God..."

Psalm 16 is a Michtam Psalm. There are six of these, Psalm 16 and Psalms 56-60. They are private meditations.

Psalm 46 is set in a time when Israel was surrounded by enemies. Our position should be to get into the presence of God. Psalm 46:1 says, "God is our refute and strength..." In the busyness of life, we need to be still and know that he is God. We cannot know God if we are running in ten different directions. Prayer begins with getting alone and being still. Then praise God.

"The Lord of Hosts is with us, the God of Jacob is our refuge." (Psalm 46:11)

"In Judah is God known; his name is great in Israel" (Psalm 76:1).

R - Remember God (Thanksgiving)

Psalm 16:6, "The lines are fallen unto me in pleasant places; yea, I have a goodly heritage."

David was on the run, a fugitive, but he remembered God and what God had given him. In Psalm 46:1 he says, "God is our refuge and strength, a very present help in trouble."

Remember all the times that you have been in tight places and God helped you. In Psalm 106:1 David cries out, "Praise ye the Lord. O give thanks unto the Lord; for he is good..."

A - Admit My Sins to God (Confession)

Psalm 106:6, "We have sinned with our fathers, we have committed iniquity, we have done wickedly."

Three words and phrases for sin are used here:

"Sinned" means to miss the mark, to fall short. It is the practice of sin.

"Committed iniquity" means to be bent or crooked. It is the nature of sin.

"Done wickedly" means lawlessness. It is the choice of sin.

David confesses his sin and the sins of the nation of Israel.

Y - Yourself and Others' Needs to God (Petition)

Psalm 106:47, "Save us, O Lord our God..."

After praise, thanksgiving, and confession, we certainly have personal needs, and we know of others who have needs. We can intercede for them.

Psalm 136:26 reminds us that "his mercy endureth forever." That's why prayer goes on and on.

PRAY.

On a mission trip to West Africa, our team was on a bus. We approached an angry crowd. They stopped our bus and started shaking it from one side to the other. A taxicab driver had been killed the day before and all cab drivers were protesting. They were angry that our bus was out. We were concerned. No, we were afraid. Then someone started praying, then singing, and shortly the protestors backed away and our bus traveled on.

In a tight spot:

PRAY

LEARN OF GOD

Record one thing you learned.

LEAN ON GOD

Lord, thank you for the privilege of prayer. What a comfort and strength.

LAUGH WITH GOD

Read and share.

A pastor told one of his church members, "I wish I had ten members just like you."

"Really?" the member responded. "I'm a little surprised to hear you say that since I often complain about your preaching, hardly give anything in the offering, and haven't volunteered any of my time for any of our ministries. Why would you want ten people just like me?"

The pastor replied, "I wish I had ten members like you, but the problem is, I have fifty!"

Day 17

LISTEN TO GOD

Read Psalms 17, 47, 77, 107, and 137.

COUNT YOUR BLESSINGS

David had a number of choir directors, music ministers, worship leaders, and tune "hysters," or as we called them in my first church, page callers. They were not gifted or skilled in music but would stand before the little congregation and call out the number of the next song in the hymnal.

David's music leaders were skilled singers and poets. Asaph was one of these men (I Chronicles 6:39).

Psalms 50 and 73-83 are labeled "Psalms of Asaph." A summary of all of Asaph's work would produce the theme of judgment of God and the prayers of His people.

Psalm 77 was written sometime after 721 B.C. with the Assyrian invasion of the Northern Kingdom and before 586 B.C., the Babylonian invasion of the Southern Kingdom.

When surrounded by problems and when the horizon grows dark, we tend to become depressed. We sometimes refer to these difficult days as the "blues." The term, meaning "low spirits," was first recorded in 1741.

Blues

Notice the psalmist here. Listen, feel his low spirit, his sorrow, his "blues."

> Psalm 77:1, "I cried unto God with my voice..."

> Psalm 77:2, "In the day of my trouble I sought the Lord: my sore ran in the night, and ceased not: my soul refused to be comforted."

This writer was hurting. He is praying but getting no answer.

> Psalm 77:3, "I remembered God, and was troubled: I complained, and my spirit was overwhelmed."

> Psalm 77:4, "Thou holdest mine eyes waking: I am so troubled that I cannot speak."

> Psalm 77:7, "Will the Lord cast off for ever?..."

> Psalm 77:8, "Is his mercy clean gone for ever?..."

> Psalm 77:9, "Hath God forgotten to be gracious?..."

He begins to question God.

Blessings

What is the answer for the blues?
Count your blessings.

> Psalm 77:11, "I will remember the works of the Lord: surely I will remember thy wonders of old."

> Psalm 77:12, "I will meditate also of all thy work, and talk of thy doings."

The blues are easy to get. The old blue devil will take you there in a hurry. He will have you singing the blues. He wants nothing more than to steal your joy, kill your spirit, and destroy your testimony. What are we to do? Count our blessings.

Recently, I found myself having a blue Monday. Enrollment looked as if it were going to be down at the college. The insurance agent said that rates would be going up. Five AC units were out across campus. Talks of budget cuts were daily conversation. I took some people to a conference and bought their dinner, and all they did was complain about how loud the music was. It was flu season, and my wife, Susan, had the flu for two weeks. Then I had it for two weeks. Over a month had passed since I'd even kissed my wife. I mean, I really had the blues. Then God's Spirit said, "Remember."

I started meditating on the past year and how God had blessed us. Enrollment was down, but still the second highest in the history of the college. We had over 100 students respond to an invitation in Chapel services that year to make decisions. We trained over 100 students in disaster relief, and on four different occasions, students served with blood, sweat, and tears in the Houston area after Hurricane Harvey. We had about eight of our preacher boys serving as supply preachers and youth ministers. The convection oven in the cafeteria went out, but someone wrote a check to replace it. We needed a tractor and mower that cost $26,000, and the WMA of Texas raised the money. The choir and golf team needed a trailer and a person drove up at homecoming with a new trailer. It was the end of the month and payroll was short $18,800. We had exhausted our resources. A check for $19,000 came in the mail.

What did you learn?

What do you do when you have the blues?

COUNT YOUR BLESSINGS

LEARN OF GOD

Record one thing you learned.

LEAN ON GOD

Lord, thank you for your grace and mercy. Forgive me when I have the blues and help me to see how you have blessed me. You are a gracious God who blesses.

LAUGH WITH GOD

Read and share.

"Have you heard of the Tate family? They're very prominent in many churches.

There's old Dick Tate wants to run everything. Ro Tate tries to change everything. Agi Tate stirs up plenty of trouble, with help from her husband, Irri Tate. When a new project is suggested, Hesi Tate and his wife, Vege Tate, always want to wait until next year. Then there's Imi Tate, who wants the church to be like all the others. Devas Tate always provides the voice of doom, while Poten Tate wants to be important.

Not every Tate is trouble, though. Cousins Cogi Tate and Medi Tate are the thoughtful types. Brother Facili Tate is quite helpful, and Miss Felici Tate is delightful. Just watch out for Ampu Tate.

Day 18

LISTEN TO GOD

Read Psalms 18, 48, 78, 108, and 138.

WORSHIP—WAR

As I entered the church building, I noticed over the entry door a sign that read "Enter to Worship." After the service, as I was exiting, I noticed that over the exit doors was another sign. It read "Depart to Serve." Since that time, I have observed other church structures with similar signs.

The New Testament writers would sometimes follow similar patterns. For example, Paul would often use the first half of a letter to emphasize doctrine and the second half of a letter to stress duty. Jerry Vines, in his book *A Journey Through the Bible,* records similar patterns.

Let me share some examples to visualize what I am attempting to say.

BOOK	1ST HALF	2ND HALF
Romans	Principles: 1-11	Practices: 12-16
2 Corinthians	Defends His Motives: 1-5	Delivers His Message: 6-13
Galatians	Explanation: 1-4	Exhortation: 5-6
Ephesians	Worship: 1-3	Witness: 4-6
Ephesians	Sanctification: 1-3	Service: 4-6

Ephesians	Riches in Christ: 1-3	Responsibilities in Christ: 4-6
Colossians	Doctrine: 1-2	Duty: 3-4
Colossians	Belief: 1-2	Behavior: 3-4
1 Thessalonians	Personal: 1-3	Practical: 4-5
Philemon	A Saint: 1-16	A Soul Winner: 17-22
Hebrews	Person of Christ: 1-10	Principles of Conduct: 11-13
2 Peter	Convictions of the Faith: 1	Contentions for the Faith: 2-3

Psalm 18 is a song by David. He wrote it on the day he was delivered from his enemies. This psalm is found twice in the Bible. It is found in the history book of 2 Samuel 22. Now it is found in the hymn book of Psalm 18. David had been a fugitive on the run from Saul. Now Saul was dead, David was king, and he could unite the kingdom. David, in Psalms, follows a pattern we have been reviewing. We see in this psalm David as a worshipper (Psalm 18:1-6) and as a warrior (Psalm 18:7-50).

Worshipper

In Psalm 18:2, David employs seven metaphors – word pictures – to describe God. "The Lord is my rock, and my fortress, and my deliverer; my God, my strength, in whom I will trust; my buckler, and the horn of my salvation, and my high tower." These images correspond to the military battle in which David fought.
1. Rock: A rock had provided protection for David as he hid from the heat and from the hunt of Saul. A rock had provided a place to stand and fight. A firm place, as opposed to sinking sand.
2. Fortress
3. Deliverer

4. My strength

5. My Buckler (Shield)

6. Horn (Strength)

7. My High Tower (Defense)

In Psalm 18:1-6, David is praising God. He worships. Then he shares how his history was that of a warrior in Psalm 18:7-50.

Warrior

Many notable warriors, such as Napoleon, would often brag about their strength and ability to conquer. David, an exceptional military genius in his own right, humbles himself and admits his need for God in battle. Psalm 18:6, "In my distress I called upon the Lord, and cried unto my God..." He had learned early in the confrontation with Goliath that the battle is the Lord's.

It really is no different today. This pattern of worship and war should outline our life. We should rise early, read our Bibles, pray, and worship God. Then we should put on the armor of God and go out to do war. Our enemy Satan is waiting like a lion to pounce on us and devour us. We cannot let our guard down or this world will eat us up. So, remember to be a:

WORSHIPPER-WARRIOR

LEARN OF GOD

Record on thing you learned.

LEAN ON GOD

Lord, we are in a war. The enemy seeks to destroy us daily. Help me to worship you first and let you fight the battles.

LAUGH WITH GOD

Read and share.

Why do gorillas have big nostrils? Because they have big fingers.

Day 19

LISTEN TO GOD

Read Psalms 19, 49, 79, 109, and 139.

ACTS OF PRAYER

As a young pastor, I desired my church to be a "house of prayer." We developed many prayer groups that met at various times. We had prayer conferences and seminars. One such was presented by a man who taught us to pray the ACTS of prayer. This simple acrostic is a great outline to assist you in arranging your prayers. Each letter contains one of the key elements of prayer.

> A – Adoration. This is praise. Prayer should start with praises unto God. These are phrases that describe who God is and what God does.

> C – Confession. When one comes into God's holy presence, there will be an awareness, a conviction of sin. Sin needs to be confessed. Confess means to agree with God that we have sinned. We have broken His law and fall short of His Holiness. We need forgiveness.

T – Thanksgiving. When we pray, we should always give thanks. We should remember God's grace and goodness towards us.

S – Supplication. Prayer certainly contains petitions, requests for our needs and the needs of others.

Another way to pray as you read through Psalms is to take the beautifully inspired words of God and pray the Psalms. Read your five psalms a day. Go back and write out your prayers. Pray the psalmist's words and your words. Let's take today's five psalms and use them as an example of how to pray the psalms.

A - Adoration/Praise

Psalm 139

I hold that David is the writer of this beautiful psalm of praise. In no other psalm, or possibly the whole Bible, do we find such expressions of the essential attributes of God.

God is omniscient. He is all-knowing. He knows our every movement. "Thou knowest my downsitting and mine uprising..." (Psalm 139:2a).

He knows our every motive. "...thou understandest my thought afar off" (Psalm 139:2b).

God is omnipresent. He is everywhere. In verse 8, David says, "If I ascend up to heaven, thou art there: if I make my bed in hell, behold, thou art there." You cannot hide from God.

God is omnipotent. He is all-powerful. In verse 14, David says, "...I am fearfully and wonderfully made..."

Psalm 19:1 says, "The heavens declare the glory of God; and the firmament sheweth his handywork." Just look around, and everywhere you will see God's work. That should cause you to burst out in praise to the Lord.

C - Confession

"Search me, O God, and know my heart: try me, and know my thoughts: And see if there be any wicked way in me, and lead me in the way everlasting" (Psalm 139:23-24).

Every prayer should contain an agreement with God that we have sin and claim our forgiveness because the blood of Jesus cleanses us of all sin (Psalm 79:9).

T - Thanksgiving

"So we thy people and sheep of thy pasture will give thee thanks for ever: we will shew forth thy praise to all generations" (Psalm 79:13).

We could never exhaust the things for which we should thank God. They number more than the sand (Psalm 139:18).

S - Supplication/Petitions

"Help me, O Lord my God..." (Psalm 109:26). God can and will do for us what no one else can. He is the one to whom we should cry out our needs and the needs of others.

Example of Praying the Psalms

"Lord, You are all knowing, all powerful. You know my downsitting and my uprising. Lord, you made me, I am fearfully and wonderfully made. Lord, the heavens declare Your glory. Lord, I praise Your name.

Lord, search me and if there is any sin in my life, convict me of those sins. I agree with You and Your Word if there is sin, and I claim forgiveness because of the blood of Jesus.

Lord, I have so many things to be thankful for. If I were to count them, they would be more than the grains of sand or the drops of water in the sea.

Lord, help me. No one else can. There is none besides You. Order my steps today, Lord. I intercede for my wife, children, and grandchildren with whom you have blessed me.

Lord, let the words of my mouth and meditations of my heart be acceptable in Your sight, O Lord, my strength and my redeemer."

ACTS OF PRAYER

LEARN OF GOD

Record one thing you learned.

LEAN ON GOD

Lord, you are holy and your word is perfect. Your words are beautiful and powerful. Help me as I pray to recall your words.

LAUGH WITH GOD

Read and share.
Why do dogs make poor dancers? They have two left feet.

Day 20

LISTEN TO GOD

Read Psalms 20, 50, 80, 110, and 140.

LEADERS PRAY

The setting of Psalm 20 is war. David was a warrior. His life was marked by war. As a shepherd boy, David fought both a lion and a bear in order to protect his sheep. As a young man, he faced Goliath at a time when no one else would fight the Philistine. With one shot from David's sling, Goliath fell dead on the ground. Because of jealousy and the fear of losing his power, King Saul chased David all over the hills of Judea. As king, David conquered all the nations around Jerusalem and brought them into the kingdom.

War was not foreign to God's people. The Old Testament is full of war stories. The books of Judges, Samuel, Kings and, Chronicles are books of war stories. The history of Israel is one of conflict. In all these conflicts and wars, the people looked to their leader. By application and devotional thought, I want to apply Psalm 20 to leadership.

In my opinion, there is a vacuum of leadership. Our society lacks biblical leaders. I see a lack of biblical leaders in the

White House, the State House, the City House, in the church house, and in the Christian house.

According to the Jacksonville College Mission Statement, "Jacksonville College exists to provide a quality education from a biblical worldview that challenges minds, transforms lives, and equips students for servant leadership and lifelong learning." This is why Jacksonville College is so important in our society. Jacksonville College is the only faith-based two-year college left in Texas and it is preparing tomorrow's leaders from a biblical worldview.

Let's look at Psalm 20 and apply its message to the kind of leaders we need today.

LEADERS PRAY

Notice the emphasis on prayers. Verse 1 says, "The Lord hear thee in the day of trouble." In verse 2, David says, "Send thee help from the sanctuary." The sanctuary was the place from which to expect power to come. In verse 3, he says," Remember all thy offerings, and accept thy burnt sacrifice."

The people of Israel wanted a king who listened to God. We need leaders today who pray and listen to God. Any decision apart from prayer is mere human reason.

Ever since World War II in the 1940s, the late Billy Graham met with every president to pray. He met with Harry Truman and had prayer. Dwight Eisenhower asked for Billy Graham's counsel before sending troops into Little Rock. Four days before John F. Kennedy was to be inaugurated as President, he invited Billy Graham to spend the day with him in Palm Beach. Lyndon Johnson, to the surprise of many, invited Billy Graham more than 20 times to spend the night at the White House. Every time that Graham would say, "Let's have a prayer," Johnson would get on his knees. Billy prayed with Richard Nixon, Gerald Ford, Jimmy Carter, and Ronald Reagan. In 1991, the night before George H. W. Bush sent troops into the Gulf War, he asked Billy to spend the night in the White House. President Bush said, "It is my firm belief that no one can be president without a belief in God, without understanding the power of prayer, without faith."

Billy Graham prayed with President Bill Clinton and George W. Bush. He invited Barack Obama to his home in Montreal, North Carolina for prayer. Billy Graham met President Trump once on his 95th birthday in 2013. His son, Franklin Graham, prayed at President Trump's inauguration.

A leader is one who prays and depends on God.

"Some trust in chariots, and some in horses: but we will remember the name of the Lord our God" (Psalm 20:7).

LEADERS PRAY

LEARN OF GOD

Record one thing you learned.

LEAN ON GOD

God, you established this nation called America and have sustained it through the years. I ask for revival, for a real movement of God across our nation. I pray for our leaders that you may work in and through them.

LAUGH WITH GOD

Read and share.
Teacher: Class, we will have only half a day of school this morning.
Class: Hooray!
Teacher: We will have the other half this afternoon!

Daily Beside The Still Waters

Day 21

LISTEN TO GOD

Read Psalms 21, 51, 81, 111, and 141.

CONFESSION

Psalm 51 is one of the seven penitential Psalms (6, 31, 37, 50, 101, 129, and 142). Penitential Psalms are songs of confession. The background to Psalm 51 is found in 2 Samuel 12. Nathan the prophet went to King David and told him a story. The story was about two men, one rich who had many lambs and one poor who had only one little ewe lamb. A traveler came by and took the poor man's lamb. David got angry and said to Nathan, "The man that hath done this thing shall surely die." Nathan replied, "Thou art the man."

To understand this statement, read 2 Samuel 11. When all other kings went out to war, King David decided this one time to stay home. He was looking out onto his neighbor's house and saw Bathsheba bathing. He sent for her and committed the sin of adultery. She became pregnant. David sent for her husband, Uriah, to come home, thinking that Uriah would stay with his wife and cover David's sin. Instead, because of his sense of duty, he refused to go home to Bathsheba and stayed outside the city gates with his troops. Since his original plan did not work, David had Uriah sent to the front lines so he would be killed.

With this heavy baggage of the sins of adultery and murder, the Lord told the prophet to confront David. David broke down and the flood of shame, guilt, and tears overwhelmed him. He sat down and wrote Psalm 51 as a statement of his confession.

There is much in this psalm, but to warm our hearts and focus on God, let's see these truths.

1. Confession

    Confession is coming to terms and admitting: "I have sinned."

    Confession is agreeing with God: "I have broken His law."

    David uses three words for sin in this passage that help us greatly.

    a. Transgression (Psalm 51:5)

        "Transgression" in Hebrew is *pesha* and occurs 80 times in the Old Testament. *Pesha* means "rebellion," to go beyond the law, to trespass.

        In the South, we are all familiar with landowners posting "No Trespassing" signs on their property. The warning is not to go beyond this point. Sin is going where you should not go. David looked too long at a woman bathing. David had her come to him and they committed adultery. Sex inside of marriage is a beautiful gift from God. Sex outside of marriage is sin. David's rebellion against God's Word was to satisfy his fleshly desires.

    b. Iniquity (Psalm 51:2)

In the Bible, there are eleven words translated "iniquity." The most common is *awon*, used about 215 times. The etymology of the word suggests moral distortion, crookedness, or perversion. Iniquity denotes not so much the act but the character flaw.

c. Sin

Sin's basic definition is missing the mark, falling short. Romans 3:23 says, "For all have sinned, and come short of the glory of God."

David's sorrow and confession was deep and real. He realized that while he had hurt Bathsheba, Uriah, the baby, and his kingdom, his sin was against God (Psalm 51:4).

He understood that he had inherited a sin nature from Adam (Psalm 51:5), yet he took full blame for his sin. Confession is not trying to explain your sin to God but to agree with God that you have sinned.

2. . Cleansing (Psalm 51:7-19)

Psalm 51:7-19 are some of the most poetic, beautiful words of a desire to be forgiven and cleansed of sin.

a. From God (Psalm 51:7-12)

David knew that there was no ritual, religion, or restitution he could do to cleanse him of his sin. Only God can forgive and cleanse.

b. For Others (Psalm 51:13-19)

David learned so much from confession of his sin that he wanted to help others. Until we read Paul's words to the Romans, we do not learn the purpose of the Law. However, David learned it here. "For thou desirest not sacrifice; else would I give it: thou delightest not in burnt offering" (Psalm 51:16). It is not the outward acts of sacrifice and burnt offerings that earn forgiveness. It is an inward broken-hearted confession to a gracious God.

Deal with Your Sin Today – With ...

CONFESSION

LEARN OF GOD

Record one thing you learned.

LEAN ON GOD

God, thank you for your love that sent your son to die on the cross and shed his blood for my sins. Thank you for the forgiveness of sin.

LAUGH WITH GOD

Read and share.
Q: Why were the teacher's eyes crossed?
A: She couldn't control her pupil.

Day 22

LISTEN TO GOD

Read Psalms 22, 52, 82, 112, and 142.

SAVIOR

Psalm 22 records a past event written by David while he was hiding in a cave. He was surrounded by Saul's armies. This was a low point in his life. David had saved a nation from total destruction by defeating Goliath. Yet, King Saul, out of jealousy, viewed David as a threat to be killed.

Psalm 22 is also a prophecy about Jesus. When we read Psalm 22, we can quickly conclude that this is speaking about more than David. This goes beyond any suffering he ever endured. This is our Savior.

More than twenty distinct prophecies from Psalm 22 have been fulfilled. Yet, the psalm was written a thousand years before Calvary. This is another example of the divine inspiration of the holy Word of God. Let's consider other Scriptures that reveal divine inspiration in this psalm.

Today's devotion may take a little longer, but it is very rewarding and refreshing to read Psalm 22 alongside the New testament passages that fulfil the Old Testament prophecies.

v. 1	Forsaken	Matthew 27:46
v. 1	Prayers not Answered	Hebrews 5:7
v. 1	Roaring	Matthew 27:51
v. 2	Prayers Not Answered	Hebrews 5:7
v. 3	Holy	Luke 23:39-43
vv. 4-5	He Saved Others	Matthew 27:42-43
v. 6	Worm – Red Colored Dye	Mark 15:15; 1 Peter 1:19
v. 6	Despised by People	Matthew 27:20-26, 39
v. 7	Laughed at Him	Matthew 27:39-42
v. 8	Mocked Him	Matthew 27:42-43
vv. 9-10	Virgin-Born Mary	John 19:25-27
vv. 12-13	Roman Soldiers	Matthew 27:27-31
vv. 14-15	Agony/Thirst	John 19:28
v. 16	Pierced Hands and Feet	Luke 24:40
v. 17	They Watched	Matthew 27:36
v. 18	Parted His Garment	Matthew 27:35
v. 18	Cast Lots	Matthew 27:35
vv. 19-21	Soul Suffered Emotional Pain	Matthew 27:46
v. 22	He Reveals Himself Resurrection	John 20:19-28
v. 23	Lord's Return to Israel	Jeremiah 31, 33; Micah 2:12-13
v. 24	Lord's Return for the Church	1 Thessalonians 4:13-18

vv. 26-27	Lord's Return to Nations	Matthew 25:31-46
v. 27	All Nations Worship Him	Revelation 5:9
v. 28	He is King	Revelation 19:15
v. 29	Every Knee Shall Bow Before Jesus	Romans 14:11; Philippians 2:10
v. 30	A Seed Shall Serve Him: The Church	Acts 15:16-17; Romans 9:27
v. 31	Proclaim His Gospel	Matthew 28:19-20

SAVIOR

LEARN OF GOD

Record one thing you learned.

LEAN ON GOD

Lord, thank you for your word. Help me every time I read it to see Jesus. You are a God of your word. Thank you for prophecy and how it encourages us.

LAUGH WITH GOD

Read and share.

If at first you don't succeed, then skydiving is probably not for you!

Day 23

LISTEN TO GOD

Read Psalms 23, 53, 83, 113, and 143.

SHEPHERD

Psalm 23 is probably the most familiar passage of Scripture and probably the most quoted. Little children can recite it. Preachers teach it on Wednesdays, preach it on Sundays, and read it at funerals daily. The patient on his deathbed requests it to be read. Families, when asked what passage is to be said at the funeral, most often request this psalm.

Let's look briefly at the background of this psalm.

Who?

David is the author of Psalm 23. Perhaps he wrote it as a young man out in the hills of Judea tending to sheep. He could have written it as an old man in the king's palace, thinking back over a life cared for by God.

What?

A song.

When?

David's life is considered to cover 1,040 B.C. – 970 B.C. He probably wrote Psalm 23 around 1,000 B.C.

Where?

If he wrote this psalm as a young man, then the location would be the Judean hills where he was shepherding the flock. If he wrote it as an old man, then the location would be the palace in Jerusalem

Why?

To offer praise to God.
Let's look at a few of the numerous outlines to this psalm.

1. Psalm 23 denotes that God is a:

    a) Glorious and Sovereign God
    b) Gentle Savior
    c) Gracious Sufficiency

2. Psalm 23 is a Testimony of:

    a) Satisfaction (v. 2)
    b) Sovereignty (v. 3)
    c) Security (v. 4)
    d) Safety (v. 5)
    e) Surety (v. 6)

3. Psalm 23 depicts a Shepherd who Provides:

    a) Provision
    b) Peace
    c) Protection
    d) Providence
    e) Presence

f) Paradise

4. In Psalm 23, we see a:

    a) Happy Life
    b) Happy Death
    c) Happy Eternity

5. In Psalm 23, we see one who:

    a) Takes care of our frailty
    b) Takes care of our foes
    c) Takes care of our future

6. In Psalm 23, we see a God who:

    a) Takes us into the glen
    b) Takes us into the gorge
    c) Takes us to glory

7. In Psalm 23, we see 7 names of God:

    a) Jehovah Rohi (My Shepherd), v. 1, John 10:3-4
    b) Jehovah Shalom (My Peace), v. 2, Judges 6:24, John 10:9
    c) Jehovah Rapha (My Healer), v. 3, Exodus 15:26, John 10:11
    d) Jehovah Tsidkenu (My Righteousness), v. 3b, Jeremiah 23:6, John 10:3-4
    e) Jehovah Shammah (My Companion), v. 4, Ezekiel 48:35
    f) Jehovah Nissi (My Victory), v. 5, Exodus 17:8-13; John 10:9, 21
    g) Jehovah Jireh (My Provider), v. 6, Genesis 2:13-14, John 10:11

Read Psalm 23, relate to the various outlines, and let it refresh your soul. A certain story tells of a famous actor who stood before a crowd and recited Psalm 23 in a dramatic form. The crowd applauded. An elderly man stood and recited Psalm 23. The crowd was silent, with some people crying. Someone asked what the difference was between the two readings. The reply was, "The actor knows Psalm 23. The old man knows the Shepherd."

Psalm 23 was written by someone who knew the Shepherd.

Who is your shepherd?
Who are you following?
Who is leading you?

THE SHEPHERD

LEARN OF GOD

Record one thing you learned.

LEAN ON GOD

Lord, thank you for being my shepherd who leads me. Help me to follow you.

LAUGH WITH GOD:

Read and share.

A husband called 911 to report that his wife had fallen while they were out walking, and he feared she had broken her leg. When asked where they were, he said they were on Eucalyptus Street. Asked to spell it, he said, "I'll drag her over to Oak Street and you pick her up there."

Day 24

LISTEN TO GOD

Read Psalms 24, 54, 84, 114, and 144.

THE KING IS COMING

Psalm 24 is a parade song. David wrote it and sang it as the Ark of the Covenant came into the city. The Ark had been hidden at Kiriath-Jearim, nine miles west of Jerusalem in the wooded hills, during the days of Samuel and Saul.

David, in 2 Samuel 6, tried to bring the Ark into Jerusalem. In the transporting of the Ark, the ox stumbled. Uzzah reached to stop the fallen Ark and died when he touched it. David got upset at God and hid the Ark at the house of Obed-Edom for three months. The problem was David tried to bring the Ark into Jerusalem his way instead of God's way. 1 Chronicles 15:2 was clear that "None ought to carry the ark of God but the Levites." We see these instructions in Numbers 4:4-15, 19-20, 7:9; Deuteronomy 10:8, 31:9.

In 1 Chronicles 15, we see David trying a second time to bring the Ark. He realized his error and had the Ark carried the right way. Psalm 24 is the song David wrote to celebrate the coming of the Ark into Jerusalem.

Later, God said, "I am tired of living in this box. Nathan, go tell David to build me a big house." (2 Samuel 7, vernacular translation). So later, when the Temple was complete, various psalms would be sung daily as part of worship.

- Monday – Psalm 48
- Tuesday – Psalm 82
- Wednesday – Psalm 94
- Thursday – Psalm 81
- Friday – Psalm 93
- Saturday – Psalm 92
- Sunday – Psalm 24

Psalm 24 was sung as Jesus rode the donkey into Jerusalem in His Triumphal Entry on Palm Sunday. I feel this psalm is a Messianic Psalm, reminding us that the King is coming. Jesus is coming again and deserves our worship. Why?

1. The Authority of the King (Psalm 24:1-2)

    God is Creator and owner of this world and everything in it. Man can divide this world into continents, countries, states, counties and cities. Men can place their names on a land deed and call it theirs. But God is the owner. Tithing will always be hard for people if they believe that money belongs to them and that they are required to give 10%. No one likes to give up what is theirs. With this viewpoint, tithing is a struggle. But when we accept that we own nothing and that it all belongs to God, then giving God's back to God's work is easy. It is not my money, my time, my house, my life. No, it is God's. God has the authority over me and all the earth.

2. The Approach to the King (Psalm 24:3-6)

Who can approach God?

- Those who have clean hands and pure hearts (Psalm 24:4)
- Those who have been made righteous by God (Psalm 24:5

  God makes us righteous and forgives us of our sin when He saves us. According to verse 5, we cannot clean ourselves. But God can. The coming of the King will not excite everyone. Only those who long to worship God and stand or bow before Him will get excited that the King is coming.

3. The Arrival of the King (Psalm 24:7-10)

   This is a beautiful crescendo building to a high fever. Who is the King of Glory? Five times we are told of the arrival of the King of Glory. Jesus the Lord is the King of Glory.

   The King is coming. Is he coming for you?

Ready or Not ...

THE KING IS COMING

LEARN OF GOD

Record on thing you learned.

LEAN ON GOD

Even so, come quickly, Lord Jesus.

LAUGH WITH GOD

Read and share.

A gladiator was fighting in the arena when his opponent cut off both his arms. But he continued fighting by kicking and biting.

However, when his opponent cut off both of his feet he had to surrender because he found himself unarmed and defeated.

Day 25

LISTEN TO GOD

Read Psalms 25, 55, 85, 115, and 145.

REVIVAL

"Wilt thou not revive us again: that thy people may rejoice in thee?" (Psalm 85:6).

Revival comes from the word *revive*. It is a picture of something or someone who was, but no longer is. When he is revived, he returns to who he was. That's why the psalmist in 85:4 starts with "Turn us, O God..." Revival always begins with repentance. Repentance is turning back to God. Nehemiah was praying for revival in his day. Today, America needs revival.

Elmer Towns and Douglas Porter wrote a book in 2000 called *The Ten Greatest Revivals Ever*. Let's review these revivals.

1. Pentecost, 33 A.D.

    The New Testament begins with a great outpouring of the Holy Spirit.

2. Pre-Reformation Revival, 1300-1500

This revival occurred among the Lollards, Wycliffe, Hus, and Savonarola.

3. The Reformation, 1517

4. First Great Awakening, 1727-1750

5. Second Great Awakening, 1780-1810

6. The General Awakening, 1830-1850

7. The Layman's Revival, 1857-1861

8. The 1904 Revival in Wales

9. The World War II Revival, 1935-1950

10. The Baby Boomer Revival, 1965-1970

I've witnessed a few revivals.

As a youth in the 1960s, I saw a movement of God among our group at First Baptist in Bellville, Texas. We had no paid staff youth minister. God prompted our youth to meet together and pray every Sunday night after the evening worship service. When parents realized what we were doing, they organized a list of homes that would hold these prayer meetings. The pattern was simple. We would depart the evening service and go to the host home, a different one each week. Our group was small at first, around ten, but soon grew to nearly thirty. We would arrive at the host home and quickly arrange ourselves in a circle. We would pray praises and thanksgiving to God. Then we would go around the room and share prayer requests for our lost friends to be saved. We would pray for each other by name. After an hour of praying, the host home would offer refreshments. We saw God save many of our friends.

When I was in college at Baylor, a group of ministerial students formed a club called AEX Brothers in Christ. One night, a couple from Asbury College in Kentucky asked if they could share with our group. As they were sharing their news of revival on the Asbury campus, the Spirit of God seemed to fall on all of us in that meeting. We all left the meeting and walked the campus, stopping anyone we saw and sharing Jesus with them. This continued for months and climaxed with a big tent revival on campus.

My first church, King Baptist outside of Gatesville, Texas, was a small rural congregation. We planned an old-fashioned Brush Arbor revival. The people built an arbor. We held services each night, and many were saved. One man of poor reputation would drive up in his car, but he would not come into the arbor. He would sit in his car and listen. On the last night, during the invitation, he got out of his car, came to me and said he wanted to be saved. It was a glorious night. A couple of months later, he was killed in a car wreck. I preached his funeral.

Later in life, I served as pastor of Edom Baptist Church. When our church building burned to the ground, we met in an old gospel tent for nine months. There had been no preparation, no unusual praying, but at the end of a regular worship service, thirteen adults walked the aisle and wanted to be saved. They were church members who realized that they had never been saved.

Since then, I have traveled to forty-six countries around the world. I've seen thousands saved in one day. On one occasion, for three to four times a day, we drove to a section of town, got on the back of a flatbed truck, and played songs. The crowds gathered, and I preached a simple gospel message. Hundreds came forward to be saved.

As a college president, I've witnessed nearly fifty come forward at the end of a Chapel message, desiring to be saved.

God has given us revival in the past.

America Needs ...

REVIVAL

LEARN OF GOD

Record one thing you learned.

LEAN ON GOD

Lord, you give revival, so I pray, "Give us a revival. We need revival. I need revival."

LAUGH WITH GOD

Read and share.

A man took his dog to see the vet because the dog was cross-eyed. The vet picked up the dog, examined him and said, "I am going to have to put the dog down."

"Just for being cross-eyed" the owner asked?

"No, because he is heavy!"

Day 26

LISTEN TO GOD

Read Psalms 26, 56, 86, 116, and 146.

PRECIOUS DEATH

Psalm 116 was probably written by Hezekiah. Hezekiah was near death. 2 Kings 20:1-2 records, "In those days was Hezekiah sick unto death. And the prophet Isaiah the son of Amoz came to him, and said unto him, Thus saith the Lord, Set thine house in order; for thou shalt die, and not live. Then he turned his face to the wall, and prayed unto the Lord..." Isaiah 38:4-5 records how God told the prophet Isaiah to go to Hezekiah and tell him, "I have heard thy prayer, I have seen thy tears: behold, I will add unto thy days fifteen years."

The psalm is very personal. Hezekiah, not out of sinful boasting, refers to himself 37 times in 16 verses. He also refers to God 15 times. Hezekiah's near-death experience erupts into a Hallelujah chorus. The Hebrew word *Hallelu* is a verb in the imperative. It is a command, translated "praise ye." The word *jah* is for Jehovah. Combine the two words, and you have Hallelujah, or "praise ye the Lord" (Yates 19-20).

Psalm 116:15 is jam-packed with truth and encouragement. 1 Peter 1:19 uses the phrase "the precious blood of Christ." What do you consider precious? A Dollar? To some the most precious thing is another dollar bill. They will lie, steal, and kill for another dollar. Why? They consider it the most valuable, precious thing to them.

Psalm 116:15 says, "Precious in the sight of the Lord is the death of his saints." Why? Replace the word *precious* with *costly,* and you quickly go to the cross. Jesus died for God's saints.

1. Death is a Treasure.

    The death of a Christian is precious because it cost God His Son's death on the cross.

2. Death is a Testimony.

    The death of a Christian is precious, for it is a reward. Paul said in my life-verse, "For to me to live is Christ and to die is gain" (Philippians 1:21). We often speak of death in terms of loss, but God refers to it as a gain. We speak of death as departure, but death is really an arrival. We speak of death as the end, but death is really the beginning.

3. Death is a Transfer.

    The death of a Christian is precious for it is God's way of transferring a soul from the physical to the eternal. To be absent from the body is to be present with the Lord.

My parents were special, unusual people. I thank God for them. My mother told me several times she was saved and baptized at Pine Grove Baptist Church in rural Mississippi. I remember my dad's salvation. A preacher, Buford Cane, from Easthaven Baptist came to visit. I shyly stood off to the side but heard every word. The preacher led him through Scripture, explaining salvation. I heard my dad pray, asking Jesus into his life. I saw my dad baptized at Easthaven Baptist Church.

We moved frequently because of my dad's oilfield work, but we always found a Baptist church to attend. My dad became financially successful, and my parents lived life as they wanted. My mother laughed a lot; my dad worked hard. They were active in their church, lived independent lives, and did as they pleased.

My only sister died of a blood clot, and I still miss her to this day. My parents never really recovered from her death. My parents both suffered strokes, and my mother was bedridden for four years. After a year of hiring two sitters a day to care for them in their home, I moved them to a nursing home facility. It was tough to visit with them. I had difficulty understanding my mother, but she never quit laughing. My dad was miserable. He could not walk without the help of a walker. He did not like the four walls of the care center. After I visited with them, I often left in tears as I prayed, "God, I know you know best. But if you took them, it would be a blessing. A blessing for them." I do not resent any money I paid for their care or time I spent visiting with them. I just hurt to see them as they were.

I received word that my dad could not chew or swallow, thus he was not eating. I went to the care facility and fed him. Those at the facility suggested I put both my parents in hospice care. The hospice people were great to help us. My dad got a little better, then my mom took a turn for the worse. Her breathing was labored. My wife, Susan, and I were at her side. I whispered in her ear, "Mother, I love you, and thank you for being the best mother, but it's okay to go and be with Jesus." She soon stopped breathing. My dad was in the same room in bed next to her. I told him, and he had a bewildered, strange look. Less than forty hours later, I received the call that my dad had died. We had both of their services together at Pine Grove Baptist Church, at the same time. They no longer suffer and are now with our savior.

PRECIOUS DEATH

LEARN OF GOD

Record one thing you learned.

LEAN ON GOD

Lord, thank you for your promise that you are always with us, even in death. I think you for my parents and for graciously taking them home.

LAUGH WITH GOD

Read and share.
Why do Eskimos wash their clothes in Tide?
Because it too cold out-tide.

Day 27

LISTEN TO GOD

Read Psalms 27, 57, 87, 117, and 147.

FEAR

Psalm 27 was written by David during the time King Saul was chasing him. David mentions fear twice. In verse 1, he asks, "...Of whom shall I be afraid;" and in verse 3, he declares, "...My heart shall not fear..."

Fear is real. Some of the common fears listed in the "Top 100 Phobia List" at www.fearof.net include the following:

- Acrophobia – fear of heights
- Claustrophobia – fear of small spaces
- Aerophobia – fear of flying
- Hemophobia – fear of blood
- Xenophobia – fear of the unknown

On March 4, 1933, the United States was facing a financial collapse. President Franklin Delano Roosevelt believed the big problem was not the absence of finances but the presence of fear. In his inaugural address, he stated, "The only thing we have to fear is fear itself." Henry David Thoreau wrote in his journal on September 7, 1851, "Nothing is so much to be feared as fear." Francis S. Bacon (1561-1626) wrote, "Nothing is terrible except fear itself." The Duke of Wellington said, "The only thing I am afraid of is fear."

Well, we all have experienced fear. Warren Wiersbe, in his book *Meet Yourself in the Psalms,* provides for us a great outline for Psalm 27.

How can we overcome fear?

1. We Are in a War (Psalm 27:1-3).

   "...Though war should rise against me..." (v. 3)

   David was at war with King Saul. People will attack us physically, emotionally, and spiritually, seeking to destroy us. Paul reminds us in Ephesians 6:12, "For we wrestle not against flesh and blood, but against principalities, against powers, against the rulers of the darkness of this world, against spiritual wickedness in high places."

   As Christians, we find ourselves engaged daily in a spiritual war. In this war, we are to remember, "The Lord is my light and my salvation..." (Psalm 27:1).

2. We Are to Worship (Psalm 27:4-6).

   "One thing have I desired of the Lord, that I will seek after: that I may dwell in the house of the Lord all the days of my life..." (v. 4).

   Wars are won in times of worship. No matter how stressful life becomes, make time for worship. Daily our minds and hearts need to be removed from this world and focused on God. When David wrote this psalm, there was no temple. The word *temple* here means "sanctuary." Our sanctuary is in God's presence.

3. We Are to Walk Out (Psalm 27:7-12).

   The scene is changing. Be it a tent, a church building, or a secret place where we meet the Lord, we are to move from the sanctuary and walk in the marketplace. Verses 11-12, "comfort us as we walk out into this world. God will teach us, lead us, and deliver us."

4. We are to Wait on God (Psalm 27:13-14).

   I confess that waiting is hard. We want it now. The secret to waiting is found in the heart. "...He shall strengthen thine heart..." (v. 14).

   In the Christian life, waiting does not mean inactivity. Waiting is preparation for the next battle. As we wait, we pray, read the Bible, and worship God. All these activities strengthen the heart.

   "But they that wait upon the LORD shall renew their strength; they shall mount up with wings as eagles; they shall run, and not be weary; and they shall walk, and not faint." (Isaiah 40:31).

God will help us overcome ...

FEAR

LEARN OF GOD

Record one thing you learned.

LEAN ON GOD

Lord, waiting is so hard but help me to wait on you today.

LAUGH WITH GOD

Read and share.

A young man arrived late to work. His boss said, "You should have been here at 8:30." The young man replied, "Why? What happened at 8:30?"

Day 28

LISTEN TO GOD

Read Psalms 28, 58, 88, 118, and 148.

TRAVELING

Psalm 118 was Martin Luther's favorite psalm. It was a psalm that gave Luther comfort when he was on the go while fleeing the Pope and government authorities. The psalm is also the last of the Hallel Psalms (Psalms 113-118).

Hallel means praise. Hallel Psalms were Jewish prayers sung on Jewish holidays. Jesus very well could have sung this psalm as He traveled those last steps to the cross. The psalm was sung antiphonally as worshippers drew near the gates of the temple for the Feast of Tabernacles.

Sukkot is the Hebrew name for the Feast of Tabernacles, or literally, the Feast of Booths. The feast varies from late September to late October. It begins on the fifteenth day of the seventh month of the Jewish calendar. Sukkot was one of the three pilgrimage festivals and was a time to celebrate God's provision for the Israelites after they finished the harvest. Males were commanded to travel to Jerusalem to celebrate this feast. It was also a time to bring their tithes and offerings to the temple. Sukkot, like all feasts, was a reminder of how God delivered them out of Egypt. This feast was not only a time of provisions but also a time to look back, a time to celebrate the present harvest, and a time to look forward to the coming Messiah.

These verses seem to mirror the last places Jesus traveled on earth.

1. Gethsemane (Psalm 118:5-7)

    "I called upon the Lord in distress..." (v. 5).

    Gethsemane was a stressful low point in Jesus' life. Israel had many low points in their travels. Slavery in Egypt for four hundred years was a low point. Seventy years in Babylonian captivity was a low point. In life, even in our walk with God, there will be low points with discouraging, stressful days.

2. Gabbatha (Psalm 118:8-9)

    John 19:13 says, "When Pilate therefore heard that saying, he brought Jesus forth, and sat down in the judgment seat in a place that is called the Pavement, but in the Hebrew, Gabbatha."

    "It is better to trust in the Lord than to put confidence in man" (Psalm 118:8). At the end, nearly every man failed Jesus. Peter denied him three times. Only John was at the cross. The Jewish religious leaders plotted to crucify Him. Even the Roman government, in Pilate, washed their hands and would not do what was right.

    When you are on the judgment seat, man will often fail you. Injustice, corrupt justice, has been in this world from the beginning.

3. Golgotha (Psalm 118:10-13).

    "All nations compassed me about..." (v. 10).

When Jesus was crucified, people from all nations had gathered to celebrate Passover. People from all nations were at Golgotha to witness the crucifixion.

People often gather to see an event. People are spectators. They will stand by on a public square and watch a man steal a woman's purse, watch a gunman rob a store, or watch a murderer gun down an innocent man. In your day of trouble, people will watch.

4. Glory (Psalm 118:14-18).

"The Lord is my strength and song, and is become my salvation" (v. 14).

Stressful days are here. Your fellow man will let you down, but praise the Lord, He is your strength and salvation.

If you are in distress today, remember God is just a prayer away. Remember that this is not your home. You are just passing through. You are a pilgrim, a stranger. You are just ...

TRAVELING

LEARN OF GOD

Record on thing you learned.

LEAN ON GOD

Lord, I know this earth is not my home. As I travel in life, help me to honor you.

LAUGH WITH GOD

Read and share.
Two snowmen are in a field. One says, "Funny, I smell carrots, too."

Day 29

LISTEN TO GOD

Read Psalms 29, 59, 89, and 149.

CHURCH

Psalm 149 was probably written by David as he entered Jerusalem and set up his kingdom. This psalm is called a "New Song." There are at least six "New Songs" in the psalms (33:3, 40:3, 96:1, 98:1, 144:9, 149:1). Revelation 5:9 says that when we get to heaven, we will sing a "new song." Let's turn our thoughts to praise "in the congregation of the saints" in Psalm 149:1.

At church, you were taught the little hand song of interlocking your fingers and singing, "Here's the church," then raising two fingers and singing, "Here's the steeple". Then you opened your hands and wiggled your fingers and sang, "open the doors and here's all the people!" It is a cute song, but it has terrible theology. It taught the church as the building, and the people are separate.

The word translated as "church" in our English Bible is the Greek word *ekklesia*. It comes from two Greek words, *kaleo*, meaning "call," and the prefix *ek* meaning "out." Thus, "church" is the "called out one."

Ekklesia is found 115 times in the New Testament, and the majority of the time, it refers to a local group.

Have you noticed the names of church? A simple internet search for synonyms for "church" reveals a long list of results, including the following:

Abbey – worship place of monks
Basilica – large Catholic church
Cathedral – church of bishops
Chapel – small area of worship
Church – a building or place of worship
House of God – place of worship

Kirk – Scottish for church

Mosque – Muslim place of worship

Meeting House – Quaker place of worship
Pagoda – Buddhist place of worship
Synagogue – Jewish place of worship
Tabernacle – early Jewish tent for worship
Temple – Jewish building in Jerusalem
Kingdom Hall—place of worship for Jehovah's Witnesses
Wards, Branches, Stakes, Temples – places of worship for Mormons

Have you noticed some more modern terms for places to worship? Most are absent of any denominational identification.

Biker Church
Carpenter's Cross
CenterPoint
Church in the Wind
Church Under the Bridge
Compass
Cowboy Church

Gateway
Harvest
Little Hope
Mars Hill
Mosaic
New Beginnings
New Hope

Fellowship	New Life
Northpointe	The Bridge
Oasis	The Rock
People's Church	The Village
Refuge	Trail to Christ
Stone	Watermark

I have a friend who referred to his church as "my little flock," a reference to Luke 12:32.

As I mentioned earlier, I was the pastor of Edom Baptist Church when the building burned to the ground. We worshipped in a tent for nine months. I've also worshipped in storefronts, school auditoriums, under trees, in boats, on buses, in beautiful stained-glass buildings, and in rundown, dilapidated structures. There is nothing wrong with having a church building. People need a place to gather. However, the church is not the building; the church is the people. To me, the definition of a church is a body of called-out, baptized believers on a mission for our Lord to make disciples. The church is not defined by a location or a name. What defines the church is the people who make up the church and what they do.

We live in a time when a lot of people criticize and devalue the church. Hebrews 10:5 reminds us not to forsake the assembling of ourselves. We need one another. 1 Peter 3:8 tells us that the church is to be:

- Compatible – of the same mind. We are to have the same doctrinal convictions.
- Compassionate – sympathetic. We are to care for one another.
- Conciliatory – courteous, humble. We should not demand our way but seek unity.

I love the ...

CHURCH

LEARN OF GOD

Record one thing you learned.

LEAN ON GOD

Lord, thank you for your people called the church and the place they have played in my life.

LAUGH WITH GOD

Read and share.

Two muffins were baking in an oven. Muffin number one said, "Wow, it's hot in here."

Then muffin number two screamed, "Oh my, a talking muffin!"

Day 30

LISTEN TO GOD

Read Psalms 30, 60, 90, 120, and 150.

PRAISE GOD

Psalm 30:5, "...Weeping may endure for a night, but joy cometh in the morning."

Psalm 60:11, "Give us help from trouble: for vain is the help of man."

Psalm 90:2, "Before the mountains were brought forth, or ever thou hadst formed the earth and the world, even from everlasting to everlasting, thou art God."

Psalm 90:4, "For a thousand years in thy sight are but as yesterday when it is past, and as a watch in the night."

Psalm 90:12, "So teach us to number our days, that we may apply our hearts unto wisdom."

Psalm 120:1, "In my distress I cried unto the Lord, and he heard me."

Psalm 150:1-6, "Praise ye the LORD. Praise God in his sanctuary: praise him in the firmament of his power. Praise him for his mighty acts: praise him according to his excellent greatness. Praise him with the sound of the trumpet: praise him with the psaltery and harp. Praise him with the timbrel and dance: praise him with stringed instruments and organs. Praise him upon the loud cymbals: praise him upon the high sounding cymbals. Let every thing that hath breath praise the LORD. Praise ye the LORD."

Psalm 30 was written by David when he dedicated Araunah's threshing floor. If this location is the one for the house of David, that would be the temple which hadn't been built yet, so it is looking forward. Some say it was written on David's attempt to bring the Ark into Jerusalem and was written between verses 13 and 14 of 2 Samuel 6 (Life Application Bible, 932).

Notice that God's day begins with evening and ends with morning. Psalm 30:5: "For his anger endureth but a moment; in his favour is life: weeping may endure for a night, but joy cometh in the morning."

God used the illness mentioned in Psalm 30:2-3 to discipline David. All of us have had nighttime experiences of sickness, sadness, strife, sorrow, and separation. We've sat in darkness in a room with someone in our minds or on our hearts. But then comes morning. "One glimpse of His dear face, all sorrow will erase. Joy cometh in the morning."

The background for Psalm 60 is found in 2 Samuel 8, 1 Chronicles 18, and 1 Kings 11. It is a Michtam Psalm that speaks of atonement. Joab was David's military leader. He was the best man for the job, and David picked him. David was not looking to Joab. David was looking to God. We need good men, and when we pick the best man for a job, we need God's help.

Psalm 90 - Some think that besides Job, this is the oldest writing in the Bible. Thus, Moses would be the author. This psalm was written in the wilderness on the journey from Egypt to Canaan and is a masterpiece of writing.

Psalm 90:2 – God is Creator and eternal.

Psalm 90:4 – God's time is different from man's. We hurry through life in our three score and ten. We are prisoners to our calendars, clocks, and schedules. We need the perspective of God—eternity. This psalm reminds us our place is to be submissive to God.

Psalm 120 is one of the fifteen psalms we call Songs of Degrees. We're not sure what that means. Was it a song for a higher choir, the best choir? Was it a song of a higher key? Was it part of the fifteen stages of the annual trip of the ascent to Jerusalem? Was it referring to the fifteen steps of the temple? (Ezekiel 40:22,31).

Whatever the background, I will let others debate. Psalm 120:1 speaks to my heart before my mind. God hears my prayers.

Psalm 150 is the Hallelujah Chorus. It is the last song in this hymn book. This psalm gives a glorious praise to God. We need to praise God now, and we certainly will praise Him for all eternity.

PRAISE GOD

LEARN OF GOD

Record one thing you learned today.

LEAN ON GOD

God, besides you there is none other. Help me to worship you.

LAUGH WITH GOD

Read and share.
Who was bigger, Mr. Bigger or his son?
His son. He was a little Bigger.

Daily Beside The Still Waters

Day 31

LISTEN TO GOD

Read Psalms 119.

THE WORD

Psalm 119 was probably written by David. Some have presented a case for Hezekiah, Jeremiah, Ezra, or Nehemiah.

There is little argument that the theme is the Word of God. The Word is referred to in 173 of the 176 verses. The writer uses eight synonyms for the Word of God.

- *Torah* – Law: 24 times
- *Edoth* – Testimonies: 19 times
- *Piqqud* – Precepts: 20 times
- *Chug* – Statutes: 19 times
- *Mitsuth* – Commandments: 22 times
- *Mishpat* – Judgments, Decisions, Appointments: 22 times
- *Debar* – Word: 22 times
- *Inrath* – Word, Promise, Saying: 20 times

Psalm 119 is the longest psalm and the longest chapter of the Bible. The verses are grouped in an arrangement of eight verses with a letter of the Hebrew alphabet over each grouping. This arrangement forms an acrostic for the 22 letters of the Hebrew alphabet.

The setting was probably a time when people as a whole were doubting the Word of God. Look at verse 126, "They have made void thy law."

The wise man loves the Word of God in its entirety. He praises God for the Word of God.

Some thoughts on key verses:

I grew up attending Vacation Bible School (VBS) every summer. Early in my life, VBS lasted two weeks. Later, 10 days. Then, a week. Now I read that some churches have VBS in one day. In my youth, VBS was for church kids. VBS was an intense time of Bible study. Through the years, it has become more evangelistic to reach the lost, unchurched children. Some parents use it as a babysitter. They send their children to every VBS in town, week after week. Many VBS programs today focus on crafts, refreshments, activities, and themes, with a little Bible study thrown in.

A highlight for me was the VBS march. We would line up by age group outside on the church steps. Three children were chosen to lead the march: one to carry the American flag, one to carry the Christian flag, and one to carry the Word of God. What an honor it was to lead the parade and carry these sacred symbols. Upon arrival inside the church auditorium, we would recite the pledges to each. These pledges are ingrained in my mind and heart.

The pledge to the Word of God:

I pledge allegiance to the Bible

Dr. Mike Smith

God's Holy Word

I will make it a lamp unto my feet (Psalm 119:105)

And a light unto my path

And hide its words in my heart (Psalm 119:11)

That I might not sin against God.

Jews were taught from an early age to memorize the Word of God. Deuteronomy 6:6-9 says, "And these words, which I command thee this day, shall be in thine heart: And thou shalt teach them diligently unto thy children, and shalt talk of them when thou sittest in thine house, and when thou walkest by the way, and when thou liest down, and when thou risest up. And thou shalt bind them for a sign upon thine hand, and they shall be as frontlets between thine eyes. And thou shalt write them upon the posts of thy house, and on thy gates."

"Therefore shall ye lay up these words in your heart and in your soul, and bind them for a sign upon your hand, that they may be as frontlets between your eyes" (Deuteronomy 11:18).

Jesus memorized the Word of God. When tempted by Satan, His defense was "It is written..."

Paul instructed the church in Colossians 3:16, "Let the word of Christ dwell in you richly in all wisdom; teaching and admonishing one another in psalms and hymns and spiritual songs, singing with grace in your hearts to the Lord."

The more we read, study, and memorize the Word of God, the more will love God. I was in college with a man whose father was an evangelist. He had the New Testament memorized, not only in English but also in Greek. I have another friend, who, to begin a worship service, will allow people to read a verse. He will then quote the previous verse and the verse that follows. Some have more abilities than others.

Some work harder than others. But there is a need for every believer to memorize the Word of God.

The Word of God has literally saved lives. I heard a preacher share his testimony. He said that as a lost, travelling salesman, he went into a hotel room with a loaded .45 pistol. His intent was to end his life. He glanced on the bedside table and saw a Gideon Bible. He picked it up and started reading. He was gloriously saved, called to preach, and proclaimed the Word of God until his death.

There is nothing more comforting and energizing than to open the Bible and read it.

The psalmist closes the psalm by saying, "I have gone astray like a lost sheep; seek thy servant; for I do not forget thy commandments" (Psalm 119:176).

He reminds us that if we forget or leave the Word of God out of our lives, we are like a dumb sheep that has gone astray. One stays close to God, the Trust of life, by ...

THE WORD

LEARN OF GOD

Record one thing you learned.

LEAN ON GOD

Lord, thank you for Vacation Bible School and all it taught me. I pray churches will plan and have powerful VBS this summer.

LAUGH WITH GOD

Read and share.

A pastor and two deacons were putting up a sign by the side of the road that read: THE END IS NEAR! TURN AROUND NOW –BEFORE IT IS TOO LATE!

A car raced past them, and the indignant driver yelled, "Leave us alone, you religious nuts!"

From the curve, the pastor and deacons heard screeching tires and a big splash. The pastor turned to the deacons and asked, "Do you think maybe we should have just written 'Bridge Out' on our sign?"

Bibliography

The following resources were a help to me in my study of the Psalms.

Banschick, Mark. "The High Failure Rate of Second and Third Marriages." *Psychology Today.* Sussex Publishers. February 12, 2012.

Bibleinfo.com. "What are the Seven Deadly Sins?"

Biblestudytools.com

Billygraham.org

Center for Disease Control and Preventions CDC Morbidity and Mortality Weekly Report. https://www.cdc.gov.media.releases.cdc.gov. February 18, 2016. Press Release.

Conners, Deanna. "Why Earth Has 4 Seasons." Earthsky.org. September 20, 2016.

Coolcosmos. "How hot is the sun?"

"Depression." National Institute of Mental Health. U. S. Department of Health and Human Services.

Elwell, Walter A. *Transgression Definition and Meaning.* "Bible Dictionary." Salem Web Network.

Ezell, Rick. Sermon "Getting More Than We Deserve". Lifeway.com. January 1, 2014.

Galan, Benjamin. *How to Read Psalms in God's Presence.* Carson, CA. Rose Publishing. 2013.

Garner, Albert. *Pearls in the Psalms.* Florida Baptist Institute and Seminary. Lakeland, Florida. 1958.

Godsquad: "Now I lay me down to sleep prayer has obscure origins." New Haven Register. October 5, 2012. Nhregister.com. Thomas Fleets New England Primer, 1731. London's Jingles by J G Rush, 1840. Google.com

Google. Speed of Earth Around Sun.

Google.com. September 11, 2015. "Texas College Syllabus asked students to refrain from saying 'God bless you.'" University of Texas Rio Grande.

Green, Keith and Stuart Townsend. Lyrics to the song *In Christ Alone.*

Hobbs, Bill. *A Study of Psalms 23.* Nuggetsoftruth.com.

Idioms.thefreedictionary.com

Jones, Len, and Dennis Daniel. *The Big Book of Church Jokes with Cartoons.* Uhrichsville, Ohio: Barbour Publishing, 2009. Permission Given.

Lawson, Steven J. Max Anders General Editor. Holman Old Testament Commentary Psalms 1-75. Nashville, Tennessee: B&H Publishing Group, 2003.

McSwain, Steve. "Why Nobody Wants To Go To Church Anymore." The Huffington Post. thehuffingtonpost.com. January 23, 2014.

Mentalhealthamerica.net The State of Mental Health in America.

Milutin, Milankovitch: Feature Articles, NASH. May 24, 2018, WEB.

Nimh.nih.gov

Phillips, John. *Exploring Psalms.* Kregel Publications.

Phillips, John. *Exploring the Old Testament Book by Book.* Grand Rapids, Michigan: Kregel Academic & Professional, 2009.

Phobia List: "The Ultimate List of Phobias and Fears." Fearof.net. July 10, 2016.

Sharp, Tim. "How Hot is the Sun?" space.com, Purch, October 18, 2017. May 24, 2018. WEB.

Sproul, R . C. "A Simple Acrostic for Prayer: A.C.T.S." Ligonier Ministries, February 10, 2014. May 24, 2018. WEB.

The Big Book of Jokes with Cartoons. Barbour Publishing, 2000. (Used by permission).

Thornton, William. "The Strange World of SBC Baptism Statistics." SBC Voices. July 20, 2016.

Towns, Elmer and Douglas Porter. *The Ten Greatest Revivals Ever: From Pentecost to the Present.* Vine Books, 2000.

Vines, Jerry. *A Journey Through the Bible*, Volume 2. Free Church Press. 2011.

Welch, Lee. Lee Welch has given me permission to use his jokes. Some of the jokes Lee has shared are from *The Big Book of Church Jokes: with Cartoons.* Barbour Publishing, 2009. Used by permission.

Wiersbe, Warren. *Meet Yourself in the Psalms.* Victor Books. 1983.

Wikipedia. "Polybenzimiclazole Fiber." Wikimedia Foundation. May 21, 2018. WEB.

Wilkinson, Bruce and Kenneth Boa. *Talk Thru the Bible.* Nashville, Tennessee. Nelson Reference and Electronic, 1983.

Wittman, Calvin. "Sermon: The Prayer Life of a Christian – Colossians 4." Nashville: Lifeway Christian Resources. January 27, 2014, WEB.

Yates, Kyle Monroe. *Studies in Psalms.* Nashville: Broadman Press, 1953.

About the Author

Dr. Mike Smith,
President, Jacksonville College in Jacksonville, Texas

Dr. Smith holds several academic degrees, including an Associate of Arts from Blinn College, a Bachelor of Arts from Baylor University, and a Master of Divinity and a Master of Religious Education from Southwestern Baptist Theological Seminary in Fort Worth. He has an earned doctorate from Luther Rice Seminary, as well as a Doctor of Ministry degree and a Doctor of Philosophy degree from Southern Seminary in Louisville, Kentucky.

Dr. Smith has taught courses as Adjunct Professor at the Baptist Missionary Association Theological Seminary in Jacksonville, and for Southwestern Baptist Theological Seminary in Fort Worth. He has served on the Jacksonville College Board of Visitors, and has also been a member of the Board of Trustees for the college.

Dr. Smith pastored churches for 17 years in Texas at Gatesville, Frost, Valley View, Edom, and Terrell. He has worked with the Home Mission Board of the Southern Baptist Convention as a church planter in Illinois, and has served as 2nd Vice Chairman of the International Mission Board for the SBC. From 1995 to 2008, Smith was Director of Missions of the Dogwood Trails Baptist Area in Jacksonville. Prior to that, he was Director of Missions at Double Mountain Baptist Area in Stamford, Texas for eight years. He served as Director of the Minister/Church Relations Department for the Southern Baptists of Texas Convention for three years before becoming president of Jacksonville College in 2011. He also teaches Old and New Testament Survey courses at Jacksonville College. He starts each class day with a devotional from Proverbs and prayer.

Mike Smith has been married to Susan Springer Smith for forty-two years. They have two children, Martha Elain Gardner and Lance Curtis Smith. They have five grandchildren, William, Emma, and Jacob Gardner, and Logan and Landon Smith. they also count as their children son-in-law, James Gardner and daughter-in-law, Ashley Smith.

His other books include:
- *Conflict: Causes and Cures.*
- *A Proverb A Day: Daily Wisdom For Living*
  (Available in English and Spanish)
- *The 5 W's of Every Old Testament Book*
- *31 Days of Vanity: Devotions from Ecclesiastes*

The goal of Franklin Publishing is to enable Pastors, Evangelists, Missionaries, and Christian leaders and presenters to become published authors. Becoming a published author expands your influence and builds your ministry. You can write the book or sermon series which God has laid on your heart. We can walk that road with you.

www.FranklinPublishing.org

Come and visit our Facebook page and be sure to like and follow us to keep up with writing tips and new developments.

www.facebook.com/FranklinPublishing

www.ingramcontent.com/pod-product-compliance
Lightning Source LLC
Chambersburg PA
CBHW070500100426
42743CB00010B/1695